BEING PHEOBE

HOW WOMEN SERVED
IN EARLY CHRISTIANITY

STEVEN C. HUNTER

ISBN-10: 1941972896
ISBN-13: 978-1941972892

Published by Start2Finish Books
PO Box 660675 #54705
Dallas, TX 75266-0675
www.start2finish.org

Printed in the United States of America

Cover Design: Josh Feit, Evangela.com

CONTENTS

PREFACE

Why the need to write another book that may be perceived as something about women's roles in the church? It's not so much that I'll discuss women's roles as much as it will be a highlighting of how women served Christ in the Scriptures and throughout early Christian history. Be sure to let that sink in, because this is primarily a historical study, I confess. Of course, I believe, as I'm sure you will agree, that the Scriptures are the primary source for Christian authority.

I'll use church history along the way simply because the Scriptures do not address every little scenario. Please don't misunderstand me. The Scriptures have primary authority in matters of faith as I see it. However, when the Scriptures may not speak about certain scenarios (e.g. women waiting on the Lord's Table), I believe that church history can serve as a guide, if not a source of authority only as much as it's subjected to the testimony of the Holy Bible.

I hold that the centuries immediately following the apostles have the capacity to present an orthodox view of the Scriptures, but at times, it may be necessary to judge church history and tradition with the Scriptures when the two are at odds. The procedure I'll use will be primarily Scriptural and then historical. However, there may be times when church history speaks without Scripture.

It's my hope that this will be a work that will edify the brethren. I fully realize that not everyone will agree with some of my conclusions. I only hope that I'm given the benefit of the doubt as to my own love of Christ our Lord. May He be glorified!

INTRODUCTION

When Paul began his list of greetings in Romans 16, he started with Phoebe. Her name means "radiant." I'd dare suggest that she lived up to that name given the description of her from Paul to the Roman church.

She was from Cenchrea, which was the eastern port of Corinth. Many have suggested that she was the bearer of Paul's letter to the Romans, so he commended her to them. She is described as a "servant" of the church at Cenchrea. The term translated "servant" in Greek is "deacon" in the feminine gender, so some translate it as "deaconess." I'll touch upon this office later. Suffice it to say that whether she occupied an official position or was just a faithful, hardworking Christian, she was worthy of being commended by Paul.

She's noted as having been a "helper" ("patroness") of many. This has been understood of her having been a benefactor, so she must have had some affluence. The term translated "helper" in English suggests that she had wealth and may have even hosted a church in her home. If this is the case, she would have, as a "helper" or "benefactor" shown hospitality. She would have had considerable prominence among the saints because of her work.

The church at Rome was to receive her in a worthy manner and to assist her. She was off doing God's work. Because of this, despite whatever prohibitions were imposed on women from the Scriptures, Phoebe was a worker. She was well-known. She did what she could. I want every sister of mine to be a worker, renowned, and to do what they can. When the woman anointed Jesus in Mark 14, the disciples quibbled about it. However, Christ said, "She has done what she could." What a worthy epithet of every Christian woman! I hope that Jesus will say the same of you. While you've often been told what not to do, look at what early Christian women did, and emulate them since the commandments of our Lord aren't transgressed. We'll examine the Bible, but we'll also look at church history. One is inspired, the other may help us understand the former. Whatever you do, take the Bible as your only source of authority.

1

THE HEAD THAT
EXALTED THE RIB

When it comes to studying women in early Christianity, I have to begin with Luke's account of the gospel. I hope you've read this beautiful gospel account. I used to avoid it like the plague because it was the longest. Once I read it and studied its background, it became my favorite. Of course, you're not reading this to hear me wax eloquent about my love of the Bible, so let's get down to it.

Luke's gospel was always included in the earliest canonical lists of the New Testament when the other gospel accounts weren't mentioned. This suggests that Luke's writing was well known in the early church. A reading of this Gospel account shows that he was concerned with the marginalized of society, among whom were women. Luke's treatment of women differs from the other Gospel writers. Consider the amount of attention he gave to Mary (Luke 1:26–38, 46–56), Elizabeth (1:39–45, 57–66), Anna (2:36–38), the widow (7:11–17), the sinful woman (7:36–50), the women who accompanied Jesus and financed his ministry (8:1–3), the healing of a woman and Jairus' daughter (8:40–56), and others. In antiquity, this amount of attention given to so many women, not to mention how those women interacted with Christ, was remarkable.

WOMEN WERE TO ENJOY SALVATION

Anna's appearance and rejoicing at baby Jesus has been thought to have been expressive of salvation being extended to women in a male-dominated society (Origen *Luke* 17.9). This was a sentiment later shared by the apostle Paul (Galatians 3:28). They were now coheirs. However, just reading about Anna doesn't give us this understanding. This is why it's important that we take off our twenty-first-century lenses and put on our first-century lenses. We must understand Luke's gospel the way the earliest readers would have read it. They read this writing, and to some, the episode with Anna the prophetess conveyed God's love for women by offering them the same salvation that He offered to men. Until this point in Jewish history, at least, only Jewish males handled keeping the Law. They were also to make sure that their wives and daughters followed suit.

WOMEN AS A POINT OF REFERENCE

When you come to Luke's genealogy in chapter three, many have claimed that either his or Matthew's genealogy couldn't be trusted since they differed so vastly. In Josephus' work *Against Apion* 1.7, the Jewish historian wrote about how the records of women were kept in "ancient tables." The priests would send in records of marriages and distant relatives, and anytime war broke out the priests would use the existing records to construct new ones. Therefore, Luke's genealogy may have been linked to Mary's lineage. Ambrose, an early church bishop, argued that the genealogy was from Joseph (cf. Matthew 13:55; Luke 2:48). Yet, this genealogy was through Mary since Mary was of the lineage of Joseph according to how ancient folks did things (*Luke* 3.2, 4). It would be like introducing my wife by my name, "This is Mrs. Steven Hunter." This was a practice for a long time, and I know some older Christian women who go by their husband's name. It may be patriarchal when you think about it, but there's no shame in it at all. This is why in Luke's genealogy, he attributed Jesus' lineage to Joseph and not directly to Mary. Luke's audience might have known this tidbit of information. For Mary to have been identified by her husband would have been common, but she was the actual point of reference.

JESUS' COMPASSION TOWARDS WOMEN

In Luke 7:11–17, we see Jesus' compassion toward women. Christ's compassion stemmed from His knowledge of the destitution of a widow with no sons to care for her (cf. Jeremiah 6:26; Amos 8:10; Zechariah 12:10). Therefore, as Ephraim the Syrian put it, "The Virgin's son met the widow's son" (*Diatessaron* 6.23). Widows were considered to be under the special care of the Lord (Deuteronomy 10:18; Psalm 68:5; 146:9; Proverbs 15:25). Care for them on the part of others was regarded as distinguishing of pure religion (Job 31:16; James 1:27). To exploit a widow was reprehensible to God (cf. Exodus 22:22; Deuteronomy 24:17). Later in the New Testament, we read from Luke's Acts an already assumed practice—a daily distribution of food to widows (Acts 6:1ff). This custom is considered to have been understood by the audience by how Luke mentioned it without explanation, so the first-century church took special care of widows. Paul also wrote about the qualifications for real widows. These included their being provided for by their families, first (1 Timothy 5:4). However, if they did not have a family to care for them, the church was to be their lot and portion.

That this widow in Luke 7 had no one to care for her was truly a sad state. Gregory of Nyssa, an early church theologian, said that Luke had given us "the sum of misery in a few words" (quoted in Aquinas, *Catena Aurea* 3.1.238). To erase her pain was Christ and His compassion for her lot in life. Once Jesus touched the dead body of her son, He would have been considered unclean according to Jewish Law (Numbers 6:6, 11; 9:6–13). For Him who had the power over death, He reversed the authority of uncleanness because of His divine compassion for this destitute woman.[1]

WOMEN WITH ETERNAL SOULS

Later on in Luke 7, Jesus ate with a Pharisee named Simon. A woman came in while they were eating and began wetting Jesus' feet with her tears and wiping them with her hair. The only thing that the Bible says about her was that she was a "sinner" (Luke 7:37). The phrase identifying the woman is a subject of debate. Some interpretations suggest that the phrase was meant to indicate that she had a reputation within the city as merely a sinner (cf. Luke 7:39, 47). Others say that she was a city prostitute—a woman *of* the city. Regardless, both Simon and Jesus acknowledged her sinfulness, and Jesus said that her sins were many. Her identity has ranged from Mary Magdalene (cf. Luke 8:2) in medieval times to Mary of Bethany (cf. John 11:1). Her unbound hair has been interpreted by some as proof of her prostitution or promiscuous sexual behavior, socially immodest behavior, but others have seen it as a gesture of grief. Promiscuity and grief are consistent with Greco-Roman customs relating to unbound hair (e.g. Medusa). Her grabbing Jesus' feet was an act of worship (Matthew 28:9; cf. Revelation 3:9) as was having unbound hair (cf. 1 Corinthians 11:15; 1 Timothy 2:9; 1 Peter 3:3).[2]

Simon didn't say anything, but he thought about this whole ordeal and wondered how Jesus could have let this woman touch Him.

Jesus answered Simon's thoughts. This wasn't the first time Jesus knew the thoughts of men and answered them (cf. Luke 5:22; 6:8). Christ's response to Simon in answer to his thoughts took the form of a parable—Jesus' primary teaching tool. Jesus often explained forgiveness as the canceling of a debt as he did to Simon (cf. Matthew 18:21ff). The issue Christ addressed was how Simon saw Him—would Simon see Jesus as a prophet or not? Seeing the woman as a sin rather than a soul prohibited Simon from acknowledging the love of Jesus towards sinners. The contrasting actions of the woman and Simon speak to two perspectives—one to an attitude of gratefulness, and the other to denial of personal sin (cf. Luke 18:10–14). Perhaps the holy life of the Pharisee excluded him from the guilt the woman had? Whatever the answer is, Jesus showed a new way to regard not only sinners but women as well.

WOMEN AS DISCIPLES

One very familiar story in Luke's account is that of Mary and Martha (Luke 10:38–42). Preachers often pose the question, "Which are you, Mary or Martha?" in sermons. This is an excellent teaching passage on taking the time to learn and be contemplative. In Luke 10:39, however, Mary is sitting at the feet of Jesus. This was the position that a disciple took. It's the very same posture that Paul took when he learned from Gamaliel in Jerusalem (Acts 22:3; cf. Luke 8:35). What's so startling about this story is that women were not disciples of rabbis. Period! They received no formal education, and the only skills they were taught were typically household duties. Moreover, if a man instructed his daughter in the Law, it was as if he was teaching her lustfulness according to the rabbis (*m. Sotah* 3.4). Women were too simple minded to learn such deep truths, so it was believed. For Mary to have become a disciple was for Jesus to have elevated women. This one small detail in this story is often overlooked, but it is a profound truth in a short phrase. Luke shows that Christ elevated women to the status of a disciple (Luke 24:10).

LUKE'S TREATMENT OF WOMEN

We could go on with stories from Luke, but suffice it to say that Jesus treated and regarded women in a way that differed vastly from how society typically saw them. When you read Luke's gospel and the amount of attention that he gave to women, one must decide if Luke was elevating women in the first century, or if he was limiting them. Had the role of women become something that needed to be restricted (cf. 1 Corinthians 14:34; 1 Timothy 2:9–12), or did they need to be exalted? Whatever the answer may be, Luke gave us a view of women that was different. The women who followed Jesus were what could make the story so unbelievable to Luke's audience. Women were not disciples of rabbis though it was not uncommon for wealthy patrons to support traveling teachers as in Luke 8:1–3.

I believe that to a degree, Christianity valued women in a society that often repressed them. This is not to suggest that their lives were completely miserable. It is to suggest that the gospel of Jesus Christ saw them differently. The Christian society viewed them as equals. However, though they were equals, they also had God-given rules to follow that were unique to their sex. They were not to usurp a man's teaching authority. Paul argued this principle from the creation order in 1 Timothy 2:11–14. If the creation order can be excused away here, then it must be excused away when Jesus taught about marriage in Matthew 19:4–6. The fact is, this was God's design, and His design had implications.

Not only do women have a responsibility before God, but so do men and children. Our individual responsibilities that are given because of sex or age doesn't make us lesser in God's sight. We serve the God of order, and all things are to be done decently and in order. This is God's design.

CONCLUSION

This chapter about women in Luke is by no means as exhaustive as I could make it. If it were, I fear I'd exhaust you by reiterating the point over and again. Luke's gospel and his Acts of the Apostles show that women had a very, and I do mean *very*, active role in the church. Because they were so active, they made an impact in spreading the gospel.

Women had various other functions in the first century. Some prophesied (Acts 2:17–18; 1 Corinthians 11:5), taught (Titus 2:3–5), worked for the church to advance the Gospel (Romans 16:1–2, 6, 12), and served (Acts 9:36). The widows enrolled in the church's register had certain qualifications that included service. One might contend that those widows enrolled were a particular area of ministry of service in the church. They were to have shown hospitality, washed the saints' feet, help the afflicted, and been devoted to doing good (1 Timothy 5:3–16).[3] Were these women pew warmers? By no means. Neither should Christian women be today.

Is the church guilty of devaluing women today? I would say that we may bear some responsibility for this. However, I fully believe that without our great, sweet sisters in the church, much would go undone. I'm so thankful for the women who serve Christ. My own wife has taught classes and spoke in ladies' days, but she exercises her gifts within the confines of God's commands as we discern them. You can serve, and you should serve, but only in ways that God allows.

QUESTIONS

1. Considering how Luke's portrayal of women would have exalted them in the first century, how might we as churches of Christ lessen God's view of women?

2. Has preaching in churches of Christ typically (in your experience) centered on what women can't do? If so, what impression has that given you of how God views you as a woman?

3. Since Jesus exalted women in his own time by elevating them to a disciple status, does this suggest that women should be exalted in ways beyond convention?

4. How careful should we be to respect women as God did while also preserving the position that He has created for them in the church which excludes preaching?

NOTES

1. David Lyle Jeffrey, *Luke* (Grand Rapids: Brazos Publishing Group, 2012), 106–07.

2. Cf. *Chaereas and Callirhoe* 8.8.15; *Satyricon* 45; *Deipnosophists* 13.590; *Aeneid* 3.65; et. al.

3. Everett Ferguson, *The Church of Christ: A Biblical Ecclesiology for Today* (Grand Rapids: Wm. B. Eerdmans Publishing Company, 1996), 339–41.

2

SHE'S GOT THE SPIRIT

When Peter preached that first sermon on Pentecost in Acts 2, he explained the miraculous speaking in tongues by citing the prophecy from the book of Joel. He said, "And in the last days it shall be, God declares, that I will pour out my Spirit on all flesh, and your sons and your daughters shall prophesy, and your young men shall see visions, and your old men shall dream dreams; even on my male servants and female servants in those days I will pour out my Spirit, and they shall prophesy" (Acts 2:17–18). There it is in black and white—the women would be prophetesses. They would join the ranks of other prophetesses such as Miriam (Exodus 15:20–21), Deborah (Judges 4:4), Huldah (2 Kings 22:14), Noadiah (Nehemiah 6:14), and Isaiah's wife (Isaiah 8:3). Some of those whom we'd know about would be Anna (Luke 2:36), Philip's daughters (Acts 21:9), and some Corinthians sisters (1 Corinthians 11:5). There may have even been Roman prophetesses when you consider the list of folks named in Romans 16 and couple that with the fact that prophecy was present at Rome (Romans 12:6).

However, these women weren't allowed to speak in the public

worship assembly. Paul mentioned the Corinthian prophetesses in 1 Corinthians 11:5, but he asked that they not speak in the public worship assembly in 1 Corinthians 14:33–35. This wasn't his being a misogynist as some have suggested. He also requested that the tongue speakers who didn't have an interpreter remain silent (1 Corinthians 14:28), as well as the prophets while another was giving a revelation (1 Corinthians 14:30). Paul asked a whole bunch of folks to remain silent in this passage, so he wasn't just picking on the women.

If they were to stay silent in the assembly, when could they speak? Well, outside the worship meeting would be my conclusion. Did you ever notice in 1 Corinthians 11:17–18 that Paul directly focused on the church meeting? He used a phrase like, "When you come together as a church" (NASB). Immediately after this, he went directly into speaking about the Lord's Supper (Eucharist), and then in 1 Corinthians 16:2 he talked regarding their meeting on every first day of the week. Between those two points in 1 Corinthians, Paul's focus never shifted away from the assembly. In the corporate worship meeting, the women—gifted or not—were to remain silent. He gave an explanation of this in greater detail in 1 Timothy 2:11–15.[1]

Having said that, I want to point out that God's design for the church wasn't to bless people with gifts only to stifle the exercise of those gifts. Rather, he wanted all things to be orderly and without confusion (1 Corinthians 14:33). When you consider that all Christians were to be subject to their church leaders (Hebrews 13:7, 17), this does not mean that a prophet could act in such a way that undermined the eldership. Children are to obey their parents (Colossians 3:20), but a Christian child's talent or giftedness did not give them a get-out-of-jail-free card to disobey their parents before God's sight. Moreover, all Christians are to be subject to governing authorities (Romans 13:1–5). This doesn't mean that the government is more valuable in God's sight. These hierarchical organizations are a direct reflection of God's creation. The world is well ordered, so we as Christians should have well-ordered lives. Even in the organizational lists of the church, apostles always come first and prophets second (1 Corinthians 12:28; Ephesians 2:20; 4:11; Revelation 18:20). This in no way meant that one's gift was insufficient or of less worth, but that God has an order in the world that would have us subscribe to chaos.

THE PROPHET IN THE OLD TESTAMENT

What are we to make of the women prophets? They, like men, received God's Holy Spirit for the purposes of revelatory knowledge. While they could not preach this revelatory knowledge in the worship assembly, you and I both know that their supernatural knowledge— whatever it consisted of—was somehow or in some way revealed even to men. However, we may also conclude that it was told in an orderly way that did not contradict God's holiness and righteousness.

To get a grasp of prophetesses, we'd likely understand them better through the role of a prophet as a whole. The famous definition of a "prophet" is typically "someone who can tell the future." That's partially correct. The terms used in Hebrew and Greek both denote someone who was God's spokesman. They were also called "seers" (1 Samuel 9:9). This was the term replaced by "prophet," and they often saw visions. Moses was called a "man of God" (Deuteronomy 33:1; Joshua 14:6), Ezekiel was called the "watchman" (Ezekiel 3:17), and Haggai was called the "messenger of Yahweh" (Haggai 1:13). A false prophet was called "man of the spirit" (Hosea 9:7). These terms are more descriptive of prophet's actions, but they were also titles.

The first full reference to the prophetic office occurs in Exodus 4:11–21. God would teach the prophet what was to be spoken (4:12). He would be with the prophet's mouth (4:15), the prophet was as God when they spoke (4:16; cf. Exodus 7:1), and God empowered the prophet (4:21). The formula of the prophetic message often was accompanied by phrases that distinguished the word—such as, "Thus sayeth the Lord." Some prophets began by saying that "the word of the Lord came" to them. In Deuteronomy 13:1–5, we understand that in order for a prophet not to be a false prophet, what they said must come to pass (v. 2). Their message was not to contradict explicit commandments from God (vv. 2–4), God would use false prophets to test His people (v. 3), and the false prophet was to be put to death (v. 5).

The first Old Testament usage of the title "prophet" was with reference to Abraham (Genesis 20:7) when Yahweh appealed to Abimelech to have Sarah returned. Prophetic intercession could be limited to an individual for physical illness. It sometimes expanded to national interests for sin (1 Kings 13:6; 2 Kings 5:1–7; 19:4–5; et. al.). The intercessory ministry overlapped with that of priests (1 Samuel 1:17) and the king (1 Kings 8:12ff).

Those oracles delivered revealed God's will for future help by informing decision-making (1 Samuel 9:6; 2 Samuel 7:1–17), bringing comfort (2 Chronicles 34:26–28; Isaiah 38:5), or warning of calamity (2 Kings 1:1–17; 6:6). The oracles recorded were given to kings; however, this does not negate the ministry of prophets to ordinary people. When counsel was given, it was often based on the wisdom of the prophet and their relationship to God; however, that knowledge was highly regarded (cf. 2 Samuel 16:23).

Some prophets, in the context of Temple worship, prophesied in song (1 Chronicles 25:1–6), while others were filled with the Spirit for such purposes (2 Chronicles 20:14–17). The heads of the three families of Levitical singers were titled "seer" (Herman, 1 Chronicles 25:5; Asaph, 2 Chronicles 29:30; Jeduthun, 2 Chronicles 35:15). Prophecy and music were sometimes blended together (Exodus 15:20–21; Numbers 12:2; 1 Samuel 10:5). Musical prophecy outside the temple worship continued after the time of David (2 Kings 3:15; Ezekiel 33:31–33). The sons of the prophets descended Gibeah while prophesying with musical accompaniment (1 Samuel 10:5–13).[2]

THE PROPHET IN THE NEW TESTAMENT

The Day of Pentecost carefully exhibited the events contained in Numbers 11:25–29. On this occasion, the elders were to help Moses with the burden of caring for the people. The elders prophesied to show that they were to help Moses. By looking at the passage, this appears to have been a one-time manifestation while the outpouring of the Spirit on Pentecost in Acts 2 was replicated with Cornelius in Acts 10. When the language of Peter's describing what happened in Cornelius' household in Acts 11 is studied, it's clear that Peter linked the baptism of the Holy Spirit from Pentecost with what happened in the Roman centurion's home. Spirit baptism could only be administered by Jesus (John 1:33; Acts 1:5; 2:33). Cornelius' household received this baptism (Acts 10:47; 11:15–17) as a promise stated in Joel 2:28–32 and repeated by Peter in Acts 2:16–18. Moses would have been happy for all of Israel to have had the Spirit and prophesied just as Paul preferred prophecy over tongues (1 Corinthians 14:1, 39).

In the New Testament, Paul emphasized the prophet's work of edification, encouragement, and consolation (1 Corinthians 14:3–4; cf. Acts 15:32). They only received partial revelation because he wrote that they "knew in part" (1 Corinthians 13:9, 12). Their messages might have required clarification and were to have been discerned by other gifted persons (1 Corinthians 14:37ff). What was interesting was that the prophet in the New Testament was not to judge his own message, because the church had an obligation to test the prophets because of false teachings (1 Corinthians 14:29; 1 John 4:1). Paul submitted the prophets to the necessity of judgment by the church (1 Thessalonians 5:19–22), other prophets (1 Corinthians 14:29), and apostolic teaching (1 Corinthians 14:37f).[3]

When the New Testament writers referred to the prophets, they were usually referred to as the "holy prophets" (Luke 1:70; Acts 3:21; 2 Peter 1:21; Revelation 22:6). Their holiness didn't indicate that they were perfect, but that they were dedicated to God and His covenant. Nathan couldn't have delivered the message to the adulterant David had he too struggled with fornication. What's important about the prophets were that they had God's Holy Spirit (2 Peter 1:19–21; Ephesians 3:5). They sometimes received the prophecy ecstatically in the Old Testament (1 Samuel 10:11; 19:24) or in a more natural way (1 Corinthians 14:29–32). The reception of the prophetic message is wholly a mystery, but we know enough to say that the prophet was captured by God's Word and obligated to communicate it to whomever God willed (cf. Jeremiah 20:7–9).

Agabus predicted a famine to come (Acts 11:27–30) similar to the one that Elisha predicted (2 Kings 8:1–2). The prophecy did not prohibit the actions of a person, but warned of their impending result should one not heed them (Acts 21:10–11; cf. 1 Kings 22:30). This resurgence of prophesying was also like OT prophecy in that it was met with conflict (Acts 13:6; cf. Mark 7:15; 13:22).

CONCLUSION

When we understand the prophetic ministry, we understand in part the work of the prophetesses. Though they were restricted from exercising their gifts in the public assembly, they were not less valuable than male prophets. God chose them just as he wanted the men to serve in this capacity, and the New Testament attests to their existence during the apostolic church.

QUESTIONS

1. How might women prophets have differed from their male counterparts?

2. What can we understand by God selecting women as prophets?

3. Since women could have God's Spirit, how might some use this as a coverall for justifying things that God has prohibited?

4. Does God's giving His Spirit to a person open them up to any and all actions?

NOTES

1. I'm familiar with the arguments that reject Pauline authorship of the Pastoral Epistles. I won't get that technical here because this isn't written for scholars, but for Christians who lack the knowledge of such things.

2. John Hilber, "Diversity of OT Prophetic Phenomena and NT Prophecy," *Westminster Theological Journal* 56, no. 2 (Fall 1994): 243-58.

3. Ferguson, *The Church of Christ*, 307-08.

3

SHE'S A GREAT TEACHER

I recall some of the greatest teachers I ever had being women, even in spiritual matters. As an adult male, I continue to learn from godly women. Any time I've taught a Bible class, and especially a ladies class, I learn from women. My Bible class teaching style is more conversational than lecture. When I ask probing questions, anyone in the class is available to offer their understanding for the benefit of the whole class. I've also learned from godly women by reading what they've written. We have many knowledgeable and talented sisters who dispense God's wisdom through the written word. Even in the New Testament, there are at least two occasions when women taught men. Let me add a stipulation to this passage: these women did not teach in such a way that was incorrect, as I hope we'll see. Rather, they taught in certain circumstances that were anything but untoward. Let's read these two stories with an open mind, always keeping in mind God's explicit commands.

PRISCILLA, WIFE OF AQUILA

It comes as no surprise that, when Apollos preached the Word without a full knowledge of all things, a woman and her husband took him aside. When you read the New King James Version, they have it as the husband and wife, but in Greek, Priscilla's name is first. Her name appears before her husband's name when they followed Paul (Acts 18:18) and also when Paul greeted them in Rome (Romans 16:3). In the Roman passage, they were Paul's "fellow workers in Christ Jesus." They both risked their own lives for the apostle (Romans 16:4).

I'd dare suggest that Priscilla and Aquila were special people to Paul. He'd met them in Corinth during a time when Jews were exiled from Rome. Paul is noted as having met Aquila and then Priscilla (Acts 18:2). People have suggested that Priscilla's name appears before Aquila's because she was more prominent, or more talkative in comparison. Whatever reason her name appears before her husband's isn't altogether known. There are a few times that Aquila's name is listed first (Acts 18:2; 1 Corinthians 16:19). However, we probably shouldn't read too much into it.

The deficiency in Apollos' knowledge led the husband and wife team to fill in the gap. They didn't try to upstage this fervent preacher by shouting out before the assembly what he'd mistaken. They did not attempt to shame him. They took him aside and had a Bible study with him. We don't know who did the most speaking, but it doesn't matter. The couple both participated in teaching Apollos. Of Priscilla's involvement, the early sixth-century presbyter, Ammonius of Alexandria, wrote the following,

> It must be noted that we must believe that women passed on the faith: see how completely desirous of salvation Apollos was, for even though he was an educated man and was well versed in the Scripture's

secrets, he did not consider it worthless to learn the fullness of the faith from a woman. He did not become conceited as if he were receiving a rebuke from a woman that "you should learn more fully the things concerning God the Word's ordaining." Therefore [Priscilla] explained to him in her teaching the things of faith, and Apollos listened and received them, for while he knew that Jesus was the Christ and the servant of God and concluded so from the Scriptures, his knowledge was imperfect, since he did not know what had been spoken and prophesied to the apostles through the Holy Spirit.[1]

What if Aquila had not been there? Should Priscilla have taken Apollos by herself to instruct him? We can talk hypotheticals all day long. The point I want to take from this story is that she participated in teaching a preacher. Though her husband was present, she took part in explaining the way of God to this preacher. Some might find this problematic, but it's clearly in the divinely inspired Scriptures. After all, if there's only a woman present to teach a man whose salvation depends on hearing the gospel, she should. This isn't usurping any role in the church, because the man is lost and not in Christ. Therefore, he wouldn't be in the church.

If Christian women are to never teach men, then they should certainly not sing in the assembly. After all, singing is a form of teaching (Colossians 3:16). The same goes with "speaking." Singing is a way of "speaking" (Ephesians 5:19), but women are not permitted to speak in the assembly (1 Corinthians 14:34; 1 Timothy 2:11–12). How are we to understand this? Well, no one would tell the women not to sing in the assembly. Wayne Jackson explains that the role of a woman not teaching a man has more to do with her exercising leadership and dominion over the man, or subordinating him to the official role of "student."[2] An early Christian, John Chrysostom, wrote, "What does Paul mean when he says that he does not permit a woman to teach? He means to prevent a woman from coming forward publicly and preaching in the pulpit; he does not stop them from teaching altogether. If this were the case … how would Priscilla have come to instruct Apollos?"[3]

There are clearly allowances for a woman teaching a man in certain circumstances, but in the public assembly of the church, they were not to do so. Some people are often confused as to why they cannot speak up in the worship meeting but can in a Bible study. Some women's consciences won't allow them to speak up in a Bible study, but the Sunday school hour is not a time of worship. It's clearly a time where only Bible study happens. This is a controversial topic that I promise you I don't have all the answers on, but we do the best we can with what we know about God's Word. If we find that we've been wrong, we ought always to correct our actions regardless of how the "watchdogs" of the church see it.

LOIS & EUNICE

When I grew up, I didn't know that everyone didn't live with their mother and grandmother. My parents divorced when I was an infant, so my earliest memories are growing up with my mom and maw-maw. We lived in a duplex in south Nashville until mom met my stepdad, whom I refer to as "daddy." It had always been just us. I must admit that their marrying was good for me. I had a dad who taught me about Christ, and his family became my family. Gram— the first person to whom I dedicate this work—was his mother. Needless to say, I have a special place in my heart for mothers who raise children without the influence of a father. I shudder, however, to think of who I'd be without the influence of daddy.

For Timothy, however, this was not the case. Both his grandmother and mother loved God and taught him to love God. Timothy met Paul and began traveling with him (Acts 16:1–3). When Paul penned his last letter to Timothy, he noted a few qualities of Timothy that we must assume his grandmother and mother gave to him.

Lois and Eunice must have taught Timothy about responsibility. The fact that Paul wrote two letters to him about his being in Ephesus and preaching shows that he was trustworthy. Paul mentored Timothy, and their relationship became such that Paul often referred to Timothy as his son in the faith. Timothy was indeed blessed to have Paul unofficially adopt him. Though his father was Greek, he had an incredible teacher in Paul that must have supplemented the groundwork laid by his grandmother and mother.

Timothy also had a tender heart. Paul was mindful of his tears (2 Timothy 1:4). Sometimes we fathers try too hard to get our boys to be tough. Timothy might have been tough on one level, but he also had a tender heart. Since Timothy was left by Paul at Ephesus, he may have been one of those listed as having wept for Paul in Acts 20:37. In the next verse, Luke informed the readers that those who wept over Paul would see his face no more. Perhaps this parting overwhelmed Timothy. He certainly loved Paul, and he didn't want to be without him.

Timothy also had a genuine faith, and Paul noted it as having been similar to the faith of Lois and Eunice (2 Timothy 1:5). In the world where everybody's a "Christian" in name, how refreshing it is to meet someone whose faith is the real deal. They don't have to pretend. They are their faith. We have a kind lady where I serve who fits a description similar to this. She is one of the most tenderhearted women I've ever met. She has such a welcoming nature and is so pure at heart. I just love Kim Moyers. I would love to have more Kim Moyers in my life. She's certainly a blessing.

If you like this small sketch of Timothy, you must give credit to

Lois' and Eunice's love for God. They trained up that child in the way he should go. He didn't depart from it. Their task was one of love. They did it without a man, though Paul would later come along and help. Timothy is known to us because of the groundwork laid by Lois and Eunice.

BAPTIZED BOYS

Something that may go along with this chapter might be when boys are baptized. In 1 Timothy 2:12, Paul did not permit a woman to teach or have authority over a man. However, if a boy is baptized, he's still a kid, not a man. Some have the feeling that women should not teach baptized males. However, if women aren't to have authority over a man, and if a man is a baptized male, then a twelve-year-old Christian can't be told what to do by his mother. Wait! Yup, you read that right.

Just because a boy is baptized doesn't mean that he's a man and that this passage refers to him. In our culture, a boy is legally a man when he reaches eighteen. That is, he's treated a certain way by law. Maturity is also a factor. What we do where I serve is that women may teach any male up through elementary school. From middle school onward, we have men instruct them. Our goal is to endeavor to please God, but also to keep the unity of the Spirit in the bond of peace.

CONCLUSION

Exercising prudence is a virtue in this and all matters. Your elders may have a different evaluation of this subject than I do, so I'd urge that you follow your elders' wisdom. I certainly don't want to transgress any of God's commands, and I would not want to lead another to do the same. However, there is an obvious example when a woman, with her husband, taught a man. Two women formed a boy into a great man, and many women are participating in bringing up boys who will be men of God. Thank you for your vital role in God's kingdom. The hand that rocks the cradle certainly rules the world.

QUESTIONS

1. Why might some make a big deal about Priscilla teaching Apollos without her husband if the story had gone that way?

2. Are we too legalistic in trying to justify when it's acceptable or unacceptable for a woman to teach a man? In other words, do we search for loopholes to remain consistent? If so, how?

3. At what point should a women not teach a male? Are we to include baptized males (boys) in that prohibition? How about men that are unsaved?

4. How might a man who is unsaved ever learn the gospel if only women are around yet the church has retracted them from teaching men?

NOTES

1. Francis Martin and Evan Smith, eds., *Ancient Christian Commentary on Scripture: Acts*, Vol. 5 (Downers Grove, IL: InterVarsity Press, 2006), 231.

2. Wayne Jackson, *A New Testament Commentary*, 2d. ed. (Stockton: Christian Courier Publication, 2012), 451.

3. Gerald Bray, ed., *Ancient Christian Commentary on Scripture: Romans*, Vol. 6 (Downers Grove, IL: InterVarsity Press, 1998), 372.

4

SHE HAS DONE
WHAT SHE COULD

A s I sit at my computer to write this chapter, we have a group from church that are on a mission trip. They left two days ago, and they consisted of many good brothers and sisters. I would bet that your congregation has mission trips, and that both men and women go on those trips. There's so much that a woman can do to advance the gospel. The Bible noticed just a few of the many who worked to advance the gospel. If women were meant to have nothing to do with the work of spreading the gospel, women wouldn't go on mission trips or door-knocking campaigns. In the Bible, there were several women who worked for Christ, and I urge all Christian ladies to do the same.

A WOMAN'S WORK FOR CHRIST

First, we meet Tabitha. She was a doer of good works and was a charitable person (Acts 9:36). Poor Tabitha had died, so Peter was sent for. When Peter arrived, the upper room where her body was laid was full of widows that she'd been kind to. They were all weeping and began showing Peter the garments that Tabitha had made for them while she lived. She literally clothed the naked. Jesus had said that if we clothe the naked, it would be as if we clothed Him (Matthew 25:36, 40). What a beautiful tribute to Jesus that she would care for those who might have been in need of clothing.

Let me ask you a question: when you die, will people weep over you? Oh sure, if you're married, your husband and children will cry. What about people who aren't your kinfolk? How many will come and cry because you were so generous with yourself and your talents that you lived a life that blessed others? Tabitha lived a life blessing others, and they were grieved that she'd died. When evil people die, no one bats and eye. When a significant person dies, there's a void in our lives. John Chrysostom wrote, "If you want to be remembered and are anxious for true repute, imitate her, and build edifices like that, not going to expense on lifeless matter but displaying great generosity in regard to your fellow human beings."[1]

So you can't sew? What can you do? Are you a full-time mother? How about mothering a child who doesn't have one? How about babysitting someone else's child? I've known of several mothers who have watched other people's children. Those mothers have always been remembered. I remember the women that used to watch me when my single mother had to work. I have a special place in my heart for Pam Pippin. I haven't seen her in years, but I've never forgotten her. Think of a talent you have, and think of how you can use it to bless others. This is an excellent way to spread the gospel, believe it or not.

I remember having to take my daughter to the emergency room one night when she was a year old. She had a high fever of 104 degrees, and we were scared. When we arrived, we filled out a sheet that asked for our religious affiliation if we wanted to put it down. Before long, someone came with a little teddy bear that a church had sewn and gave it to her. It had the church's name on it. Also, when my mother was in the hospital for an aneurysm, I couldn't have imagined going to get something to eat. In the waiting room, a good church had a basket labeled with their name on it and it had snacks. On both of these occasions, I didn't know the individuals, but I knew the people. They were God's people and members of His church. Your name may never be written on a page, but it can certainly be written in someone's heart. Sometimes it's the little things that matter the most in some of the most crucial moments.

LABORING ALONGSIDE AN APOSTLE

In Romans 16, Paul mentioned several women and almost seemed to sing their praises. I've already touched on Phoebe in the introduction, as well as Priscilla in the previous chapter. Paul also identified Mary (Romans 16:6), Junias (Romans 16:7), Tryphaena, Tryphosa, and Persis (Romans 6:12). All of these women are identified as workers. We don't know the exact nature of their work, but we'll see what some early Christians suggested.

The early church theologian Origen wrote that Mary and the other women worked when they "[taught] children how to behave, when they love their husbands, when they feed their children, when they are modest and chaste, when they keep a good household, when they are kind, when they are submissive to their husbands, when they exercise hospitality, when they wash the feet of the saints, and when they do all the other things which are allotted to women in the Bible."[2] Persis was said to have "worked hard in the Lord" (Romans 16:12). Wouldn't you like to have known what she did that was such hard work? I know I would. Paul knew and God knew. That's all that matters. When we talk about women working for the Lord, we must remember not to work for the praise of other people (cf. Galatians 1:10). Jesus warned against doing things for that reason in the Sermon on the Mount (Matthew 6:1ff). He preferred that we not sound the bullhorn when we do good things.

Paul mentioned these women. They worked. They were vital to the spreading of God's Gospel. What might God write about you and what you've done for the cause of Christ? How have you served? How have you blessed another life?

A summer ago, we had a youth group from Missouri do mission work in our neighborhood. We have ample resources, but we wanted to help since we knew the youth minister so well. We saw to it that they were housed and fed. A couple of days in the week, the whole youth group went door knocking in our back yard. We traveled in pairs just like Jesus sent out His disciples, two-by-two. What made this so impressive to me was that not just any youths could go on this trip, but only the best of the best. They had to take a test and pass it to go.

I was told that they all had been taught how to carry on a conversation and even a Bible study. Talk about impressive! What's so sad about this is that it should be more common than impressive. Nevertheless, the girls traveled in groups for safety while an adult or two walked in the middle of the road. The teens did it all. I was with an adult and we had two groups of girls. I was so astonished and grateful to see these young sisters go up to a door, knock, and engage a person in a discussion and invite them to church.

I don't know if that's anything near what these women in Romans 16 did, but I can only wonder. When we read this chapter and see all the names Paul listed of women, I can't help but wonder how our views about women in the church may be wrong because we're so conservative and play things too safe. These women were more engaged than what we could probably imagine. They knew what God expected of them, and what they were not to do, so they did what they could.

BEING A WORKER FOR THE LORD

I've always been of the opinion that competence breeds confidence, so I'd suggest that you know your Bible. It has seemed to me that the hardest working women in the Lord's church are those who are intimately acquainted with God's Word. That's what has led them to action. When they are ignorant of God's Word, they are insecure, as are men, and won't step out of their comfort zone. Life begins at the end of your comfort zone. You'll find yourself on cloud nine if you grow in the grace and knowledge of the Lord (2 Peter 3:18).

Something that I've lately come to appreciate is the work that two sisters are doing in their local jail system. One particular sister works with a group of Christians and she and a few others minister to female inmates. They study the Bible with them and offer them hope when they certainly need it. They have baptized several inmates, and their plan is to return these new Christians to society as better people. Another woman I know of does a similar work. What's unique to her work in a jail ministry is that she helps connect leaving inmates with faithful churches so that they have a support system and mentorship. These women do a work that most won't do because of their competence and sense of duty. Prison ministry may not be for you, but sitting in a pew and doing nothing is not God's plan for anyone.

There are the standard duties and works that a woman can engage in—being a Bible teacher, cooking for shut-ins or those having surgeries, setting up and tearing down for special events, cleaning, etc. Of course, some want more. They wish to do something different, and I respect that ambition. I'm one of those "do something unique" people myself. You want to make sure that you leave your mark, that you make a difference. Making a difference in Christ's kingdom doesn't always require doing something different as much as it requires you to do the best at whatever you do. You can teach, cook, or any of the other typical ways of service, but you can do it differently from others. When my wife was out of commission after having an operation, one sweet sister brought us a meal. What's unique is that she was not in splendid health herself, and if anything, we should have served her. However, she came by on a Saturday all dressed up and made up. She had spent the morning toiling to make sure that one of her preachers was fed. The fact that she did it when she might not have felt like it made us all the more grateful. I'm so thankful for Jeanetta Lawrence and the many others who have fed us when my wife was out of commission.

CONCLUSION

As with any work, you can feel like you're not doing any good. Remember that "your labor is not in vain" (1 Corinthians 15:58). You may plant or water, yet only God will give the increase in his time.

QUESTIONS

1. Does the prohibition against women preaching lead many women to believe that preaching is the only way to serve Christ?

2. Why is the work of ministry often limited to what's seen publicly, rather than what takes place when no one sees?

3. What are the tasks that women could do that aren't necessarily seen as traditional female tasks (e.g. cooking, etc.)?

4. Is it ever OK for a woman to be a minister of a church? If so, when?

NOTES

1. Martin, Ibid., *Acts*, 116.

2. Bray, *Romans*, 371.

5

WEDDED TO JESUS

We all know a few single Christians whom everyone is determined to hook up with someone else. It's like watching *Fiddler on the Roof* as the song "Matchmaker" plays in the background. A good friend of mine and fellow preacher is single and in his thirties. I asked him about someone special in his life, and he said that he was too busy to worry about it. When considering all that he and some other single Christians do for the Lord, those who are married ought to just let them be. No one is weird or some sort of alien if they chose to remain unwed.

Most Christians have good intentions. They want the single person to be like them in the sense that they are married and have families. Perhaps they want the same happiness for their single friends that they have. Hopefully, none of them wants their single friends to share in their misery given how some married folks talk. Nevertheless, if a Christian has chosen to remain single, they're in good company.

In the early church, there used to be a host of people devoted to virginity and chastity. They did this because it was how Jesus lived.

Christ had no wife, despite recent scholarship and archeological finds of a fragment where His "bride" is mentioned. No, the true bride of Christ is His church. He had no earthly wife, but He didn't object to marriage. Rather, He devoted Himself to God's will fully and lived a life of chastity. In the New Testament and early Christianity, a group of women known as "virgins" emerged with the same goal in mind.

UNDERSTANDING THE GOAL OF THE VIRGINS

During the Second Temple Period (530 BC – AD 70) a group of ascetics existed in Alexandria, Egypt known as the "Therapeutae." The Jewish philosopher Philo (c. 20 BC – AD 50) wrote about them in his work *Contemplative Life*. Their name meant "healers," "worshipers," or "miracle workers."[1] This group was composed of both men and women devoted to the ascetic life and had practices later reflected in the Christian monastic communities. Eusebius, the fourth-century church historian, believed that this group was actually a Christian group despite the name "Christian" not having yet been used. They were devoted to contemplation, fasting, prayers, Scripture reading, and good works. Whether or not they were a precursor to the monastics is unknown, but the similarities are hard to deny. This was, however, a Jewish group. Since it was composed of males and females, they renounced marriage and were often separated according to their sex. They devoted themselves to, as Philo puts it, the contemplative life. Many early church fathers identified Mary, in the story of Mary and Martha in Luke's writing, as desiring the contemplative life when she chose to sit at Christ's feet and learn rather than serve.

Ancient people differed in their view of contemplation from twenty-first-century people. If we're like Mary, we desire to learn, but not to the neglect of service. Ambrose, the fourth-century bishop, exhorted, "Let the desire for wisdom lead you as it did Mary. It is a greater and more perfect work" (*Luke* 7.85–86). Jesus pointed out that "Mary has chosen the good portion, which will not be taken away from her" (Luke 10:42).

What we have here is a distinction between the contemplative and active life as it was defined in the medieval period of Christianity. When John Calvin came on the scene, he emphasized the active life while calling the contemplative life "wickedly perverted."[2] What Mary was doing was actually a leisurely activity. The term "leisure" in Greek is *skole*, in Latin *scola*, and in English "school." It does not mean a place of learning as we understand it, but "leisure."[3]

> [...]the value we set on work and on leisure is very far from being the same as that of the Greek and Roman world, or of the Middle Ages, for that matter— so very different that the men of the past would have been incapable of understanding the modern conception of work, just as we are unable to understand their notion of leisure simply and directly, without an effort of thought.[4]

Ecclesiastes is clear about overworking. To the one who pleases Him, God gives wisdom, knowledge, and joy. To the sinner He gives the business of gathering and collecting (Ecclesiastes 2:26; cf. 2:21; 5:15). All toil and skill in work resulted from a man's envy of his neighbor (Ecclesiastes 4:4). God doesn't say *not* to work or *never* to work, but there are times when work is unnecessary. All we do by an excess of work is maintain a standard of living on earth when we should be preparing for the life in heaven promised to us by Christ. There will always be unfinished work, and as one preacher said, "I've never had anyone tell me when they were dying that they wished they'd spent more time at the office." Where do you think they wished they'd spent more time? Our society prides manual labor to a ridiculous degree. "Man seems to mistrust everything that is effortless; he can only enjoy, with a good conscience, what he has acquired with toil and trouble; he refuses to have anything as a gift."[5] We live to work more so than work to live. Even the observance of the Lord's Day can become as mechanical as the work day.

We work to create leisure and not the other way around. Leisure may be directly found within the Sabbath—a term that means "cessation." When God instituted the Sabbath, He did so in retrospect of His work of creating the world (Exodus 20:9–11). While the Christian dispensation is not bound by the Sabbath law per se, there is a principle to be found within the Sabbath—that of cessation from labor for the purposes of contemplation (cf. Psalm 46:10). After all, the end of life for the Christian is meant for a Sabbath from labor (cf. Hebrews 3:7–4:13). This contemplative life was the aim of the virgins. They worked, but only for what they needed in order to live.

VIRGINS IN THE NEW TESTAMENT

Virginity was a two-way street, but when talking about church history it applied to females. This isn't to suggest that males weren't virgins, but the term itself is etymologically feminine. In 1 Corinthians 7, there was a whole lot of talk about marriage and abstinence. Some people thought it better to remain unwed. Actually, there might have likely been a competition as to who was more holy given all the troubles Paul addressed in his first Corinthian letter. The first verse of chapter seven begins by Paul writing, "Now concerning the matters about which you wrote." That tells us that this was a debated topic that needed a real, spiritual conclusion. Who better than an apostle to answer the conundrum? Here's a basic outline of 1 Corinthians 7.

- (7:1–2) Paul writes about remaining abstinent, but because of immoralities, each man is to have his own wife and each woman is to have her own husband in order to avoid sin.

- (7:3–5) Some married couples were apparently abstaining from sex for spiritual reasons, but Paul urged them no to refrain for too long lest they are tempted and succumb to temptation.

- (7:6–7) Paul wished that all were abstinent as he was, but realized that abstinence was a gift that only some were able to exercise to God's glory.

- (7:8–9) Those unmarried and widowed should remain abstinent, but it's no sin if they married to avoid transgressing.

- (7:10–16) Some were in mixed marriages. One partner was a Christian while their spouse was not. The Christian spouse believed it better to divorce their pagan spouse to best serve Christ, but Paul urged that they remain married so that they can possibly win their spouse to the Lord. However, if an unbelieving spouse departed because of the believing spouse's faith, the believer was under no obligation to pursue the unbeliever.

- (7:17-24) Paul uses the example of how one lived when called to obey the gospel as a standard for how they should continue living. If they were married when called—though he doesn't refer to marriage in his list—they should remain so. If they were circumcised, enslaved, free or whatever, they should remain as they were when they obeyed the gospel. The last thing that Paul wanted was for Christian liberty to serve as a basis for a person being arrogant and rejecting any particular status. Imagine if the believing spouse divorced the unbelieving spouse because of their unbelief. It would come across as elitism and exclusion rather than love and patience with the unbeliever. Since the gospel is the message of love, the believer should be tolerable of the unbeliever insofar as their faith isn't harmed. Likewise, the slave should not pridefully reject his or her master's headship, and the uncircumcised should not seek circumcision. Be as you are when called. Don't be haughty as a Christian, because haughtiness is anti-Christian.

- (7:25–38) Marrying was not a sin, but remaining single for the Lord's sake was preferred. Marriage brought with it the worry for matters of the home which hindered one from doing all that they could do for God. However, to marry is fine in God's sight.

- (7:39-40) When a woman became a widow—and presumably when a man might become a widower—they would do better to remain single. Yet, if they decided to marry again, it should be in the Lord. This is possibly a reflection upon the early admonition that a believing spouse shouldn't divorce an unbelieving spouse.

So you see that, even in the first century, some were concerned with chastity. Paul admitted that it was preferred, but not required. Marriage was certainly a part of God's design (cf. 1 Timothy 4:1–3; Hebrews 13:4). Some, however, chose to deny themselves and take up their crosses by living a single life devoted to contemplation and service to God.

CONCLUSION

There's a sister at a church where I once preached who had never been married. She was in her sixties or seventies when I was there, but she was a tireless worker in the church. She would often take other women to their doctors' appointments and run their errands. One other sister had a mother in her nineties who required around-the-clock care. She would often become tired, and this sweet sister, Saralu White, would relieve her and stay with that woman's mother. Saralu may not have been an ancient definition of a virgin, but she was an unmarried woman devoted to her faith. Saralu continues to do things for others. She's well-versed in her Bible, and she also reads other books that help her understand her Bible. She has lived a fulfilled life of service. She has lived the life of the ancient virgin in a modern way.

QUESTIONS

1. Why do well-meaning Christians always try to fix someone up to be married?

2. Why do we not consider singleness as something that could benefit some people?

3. Has the church ignored certain parts of Scripture in favor over others? When was the last time you heard a sermon against gluttony or for virginity?

4. Why aren't Christians as spiritual as those in the first century who were willing to sacrifice a family life in service to Christ?

NOTES

1. Everett Ferguson, *Backgrounds of Early Christianity*, 3d. ed. (Grand Rapids: Wm. B. Eerdmans Publishing Company, 2003), 530.

2. Jeffrey, *Luke*, 152-53.

3. Josef Pieper, *Leisure: The Basis of Culture*, trans. Alexander Dru (San Francisco: Ignatius Press, 1963), 19–20.

4. Ibid., 22.

5. Ibid., 35–36.

6

THE LONELY WIDOW WOMAN

There are sweet sisters where I serve whose husbands have gone on to their eternal rest. Some of these women are the hardest workers we have in the church. One organizes several events and is on the boards of a few para-church committees, and the other is an edifier beyond what any preacher could be. Both of these widows are self-supporting, though. Their husbands made sure that they were taken care of in the event of their deaths. However, these godly women haven't been misers with their funds, but have been blessings in the life of others by using their talents, and probably even their fortunes, to the benefit of God's glory.

Widows in the New Testament, however, were a different story. They were, if without the support of families, to be supported by the church. When you read 1 Timothy 5:3–16, there were a few points about who was a legitimate widow vs. one who was not. The real widow was one who not only lost her husband, but had distanced herself from any sort of romantic relationship with men altogether.[1] For she had set her hope on God. Should a woman wish to remarry, she was allowed to do so (1 Corinthians 7:39), but could not be counted as a widow. The younger widows were to remarry lest they burn with passion and sin. Moreover, there's something about an older widow who has the maturity and solidarity that the church found advantageous.

These women were not just plopped in a chair and left to rot. No, they were utilized in God's work. They were able to do things that other women may not have been capable of doing. Our notion of widowhood differs from the early church's notion. In the early church, poverty and hunger were often associated with the widow. Thanks to retirements, 401Ks, pensions, and Social Security, this is not as much a reality in our society as it was in the first century. I couldn't imagine a worse lot in life for a woman than that. Feminists would snarl at that comment, but I still have the old fashioned values of believing that a man should make sure that his family is cared for beyond his life as much as he can. Widows who were truly widows in the first century and beyond were a group of workers for God.

THE WIDOW IN ANTIQUITY

In Roman times, the woman who married only once was admired, despite her having an opportunity to marry again should her husband die. Caesar Augustus, however, passed the *Lex Julia* (17–18 BC) and the *Lex Papia Poppaea* (AD 9) which demanded that widows remarry or face penalties. In the Roman Empire, widows made up a large number of the poor, but Christianity's view towards widows changed the landscape throughout the whole empire and the known world. "Historians suggest that the church made a significant contribution to the amelioration of poverty in antiquity by supporting widows."[2]

As stated above, widowhood—real widowhood in the church— was often associated with poverty. A greater percentage of widows were exposed not only to poverty, but death as well. Women were more dependent on men in those days. Today, however, women can go to school and receive an education to work outside the home. Then, it was vastly different. Even widows who had means were often victims of predators. John Chrysostom wrote about his mother's widowhood and the exposure she faced as a woman with means.

> For no words are adequate to describe the tempest-tossed condition of a young woman who, having but lately left her paternal home, and being inexperienced in business, is suddenly racked by an overwhelming sorrow, and compelled to support a load of care too great for her age and sex. For she has to correct the laziness of servants, and to be on the watch for their rogueries, to repel the designs of relations, to bear bravely the threats of those who collect the public taxes, and harshness in the imposition of rates. And if the departed one should have left a child, even if it be a girl, great anxiety will be caused to the mother, although free from much expense and fear: but a boy fills her with ten thousand alarms and many anxieties every day, to say nothing of the great expense which one is compelled to incur if she wishes to bring him up in a liberal way [liberal arts education]. None of these things, however, induced me to enter into a second marriage, or introduce a second husband into thy father's house: but I held on as I was, in the midst of the storm and uproar, and did not shun the iron furnace of widowhood. My foremost help indeed was the grace from above; but it was no small consolation to me under those terrible trials to look continually on thy face and to preserve in thee a living image of him who had gone, an image indeed which was a fairly exact likeness. (*Sac.* 1.5)

While widows, rich or poor, were often prone to mistreatment, the church certainly did its duty. In the Roman church, Eusebius informs us that over 1,500 widows were supported (*Eccl. Hist.* 6.43). If we think about that number from one church, we can only assume the amount of widows supported by the church during this era as a whole. Yet, those widows were also vital to the work of the church, though they received support.

THE OFFICE OF THE WIDOW?

You're probably shaking your head at the heading of this section. "The office of a widow?" Yes, there was actually an office of the widow in later church history that ranked alongside bishops, presbyters, and deacons. The third-century theologian Origen identified the position of the widow as a legitimate part of the clerical order.[1] Everett Ferguson writes, "An enumeration of definite qualifications, comparable to what is done in regard to bishops and deacons in [1 Timothy] chapter 3, is a clear indication of a distinct class beyond the 'real widows.'"[4] He goes on to note that the qualifications of widows in 1 Timothy 5:9–13 has corresponding counterparts that allowed them to serve the church. For example, they were to have raised their own children so that orphans could be placed in their care. Since they were to have been hospitable and washed the saint's feet, they could house visiting or traveling Christians and provide them with accommodations. If they helped the afflicted, they could nurse the sick and needy. If they weren't gossips or busybodies, they could teach and admonish younger women.[5]

Later Christian literature demonstrates that there was an order of widows appointed to certain tasks in church history.

Honour those [who continue] in virginity, as the priestesses of Christ; and the widows [that persevere] in gravity of behaviour, as the altar of God. (Ignatius *Spurious* 9)

Philo and Agathopus the deacons salute you. I salute the company of virgins, and the order of widows; of whom may I have joy! (Ibid 15)

Innumerable commands such as these are written in the holy Bible appertaining to chosen persons, some to presbyters, some to bishops, some to deacons, others to widows, of whom we shall have another opportunity of speaking. (Clement *Instructor* 3.12)

Ignatius of Antioch was a church bishop who was martyred in the first decade of the second century. Furthermore, church history suggests that he was a student of the apostle John and that Peter appointed him as a leader in the church at Antioch. Regardless of the historicity of who he was and what he did, his spurious letter identified the office of a widow alongside that of the virgin. Whereas the virgins had committed themselves to a chaste life in Christ, the widows were also a recognized order within the church who had functions of Christian service. The order of the widows was attributed to Peter when he used to reside in Antioch.[6]

Clement of Alexandria was a theologian in Egypt who taught at a school of theologians and priests in the late second century. He recognized certain commands about what appears to be the clerical order in early Christianity. Among this decree of the clergy, he listed the widows who may suggest that they too were an organized office within early Christianity. What this shows, when you look at a map, was that the order of the widows reached from the north of Jerusalem all the way down to Egypt in the early centuries of the church. In addition to their duties listed above, they evangelized pagan women.

CONCLUSION

Something that I've wondered about of lately is why the church doesn't support widows like they did in the first century. Now, church history aside, it's clear that the first-century church helped widows differently than we might today. In Acts 6, an entire dispute arose over the daily allotment of food. This passage speaks volumes about what the church might have done. It was mentioned by Luke as a foregone conclusion and something understood by the first Christians. Those who were truly widows were to be supported by the church. However, what so often happens today is that a widow is helped with groceries here or there, and then told she can't be sustained forever by her congregation. I wonder if God would be pleased with how churches support, or don't support, widows as the first-century Christians did. Cynthia Dianne Guy wrote in her book *What About the Women?*, "The church has not continued the practice of widow enrollment."[7]

I realize, as you do, that we have government programs that do this to some degree. But we should still follow God's ways rather than man's, shouldn't we? The law says that a person becomes an adult when they reach the age of eighteen, but does that mean that they're no longer obligated to honor their father and mother? The law also says that killing unborn babies is okay, as is homosexual marriage, but does that mean we should abandon God's ruling on these issues? The government also has programs for the poor like welfare and food stamps, but many of our churches still have benevolent programs. Why? Because we realize that we as Christians have a responsibility.

Those widows who are truly widows should receive support from the church. If there isn't enough money, I'm sure missionaries would understand us pulling back our funds, as would the youth group and others. We should show that pure and undefiled religion that James mentioned (1:26–27). There was a reason why these saintly women were often referred to as "altars of God" by early Christians, and it was because of just how precious they were to God.

QUESTIONS

1. Does your church have a widow's role? If not, why?

2. Do we see the work of widows as a ministry to the church?

3. How close to the Bible is our conception of the office of widows?

4. What could we do to better attend to the needs of widows as a church and as individual Christians?

NOTES

1. John Chrysostom *Homilies on 1 Timothy* 13.

2. *Encyclopedia of Early Christianity*, 2d. ed., s.v. "widows."

3. *Homilies on Luke* 17.10. See also Tertullian *To His Wife* 1.7.

4. *The Church of Christ*, 340.

5. Ibid.

6. Ps.-Clement *Recogn.* 6.15.

7. Cynthia Dianne Guy, *What About the Women?: A Study of New Testament Scriptures Concerning Women* (Nashville: Gospel Advocate Company, 2005), 91.

7

SUGAR-MOMMA

S he considers a field and buys it" (Proverbs 31:16). Some women in antiquity had means. They may not have been capable of doing all that the men did, but they were certainly able to contribute financially to the work of the Gospel. Paul wrote that God gives His grace to each person as He saw fit. One of those gifts he mentioned was the ability to give. Paul encouraged the Roman Christians to use their gifts in proportion to their faith and wrote, "He who gives, with liberality" (Romans 12:8). Not everyone is endowed with the means to give as much as they'd like, but some are materially blessed and able to do their giving to God's glory.

Several women in the New Testament were patronesses. That is, they used their material wealth in service to God. The term is translated as "patron" (ESV), "benefactor" (NRSV), or "helper" (NKJV). It is only used in the New Testament of Phoebe in Romans 16:2. Theodoret of Cyr, a fifth-century bishop, argued that Phoebe may have housed Paul and offered him hospitality while he was there.[1] Here's what we read from Romans 16:2, "That you may receive her in the Lord in a manner worthy of the saints, and assist her in whatever business she has need of you; for indeed she has been a helper of many and of myself also" (NKJV). Whatever the indication of her patronage was, she had left an indelible impression on Paul. However, she wasn't the only women of her kind. Though the term used for her in the New Testament isn't used to describe others, there were certainly others.

FEMALE PATRONAGE IN ANTIQUITY

Patronage was not solely a female enterprise. In Luke, a Roman centurion had built a synagogue for the Jews and obtained their favor because he loved the Jewish people (Luke 7:1–5). One purpose behind private benefaction was for the benefactor to make good political and economic decisions on behalf of a town that they'd poured their money into. The success of the city directly correlated to the success and honor of the contributor.

When Rome entered into civil war in the first-century BC, some fathers, sons, and brothers were either fighting in the war, dead, or forced to live in exile. The result of this, somewhat like in the United States during World War II, was that women controlled the family fortunes. This permitted them to be influential unlike before. When we understand this, it helps us comprehend the prominence of the women in the Macedonian churches (Acts 16:14–15; Philippians 4:2–3).

However, the benefactor relationship was usually about give and take. This is not what Christian patronage was all about. In antiquity, patronage was about the patron having influence and status over the recipient of their funds. If this were the case, then Paul would not have had to commend Phoebe to the Roman church since he would have been lower in social ranking than her. Nevertheless, Paul was the one who yielded, not a greater social status, but more significant influence because of his apostolic office. Phoebe was merely the generous servant who had aided Paul and possibly the church at Cenchrea.[2]

While all of this background doesn't exactly apply to the patronage of Christian women towards other Christians, it can be helpful to understand patronage in antiquity. Patronage in Roman society has been shown by historians to have been more prominent than one might think. More than that, it was actually imperative to the Roman economy despite it not being regulated by law. This was solely an honor/shame-based system—one that found a real home in Christianity.

WOMEN WITH MEANS IN THE NEW TESTAMENT

I've already mentioned that women financed Jesus' ministry.

> Now it came to pass, afterward, that He went through every city and village, preaching and bringing the glad tidings of the kingdom of God. And the twelve *were* with Him, and certain women who had been healed of evil spirits and infirmities—Mary called Magdalene, out of whom had come seven demons, and Joanna the wife of Chuza, Herod's steward, and Susanna, and many others who provided for Him from their substance. (Luke 8:1–3)

Let's note that Jesus traveled in mixed company (cf. 1 Corinthians 9:5) which would have portrayed spiritual equality in a society that thought of the fairer sex as inferior. Some of these women had been healed by Him, so as they were able, they provided for Him and the apostles from their means. I love how William Barclay depicts members of this entourage. Joanna, the wife of Chuza, would have been a lady of King Herod's court, while Mary Magdalene had a dark past. "It is one of the supreme achievements of Jesus that he can enable the most diverse people to live together without in the least losing their own personalities or qualities."[3] In our days when church women, Christian sisters, sometimes bite and claw at one another over superficial reasons, we see two women from diverse backgrounds working together in harmony. Christ ought to be a source of unity, not contention. In Him, all social and financial statuses are nothing. Also, Luke recorded elsewhere that many women of some social standing became Christians (Acts 7:4, 12).

Next, we come to note some women who housed churches in their homes. This suggests that they had houses large enough for several Christians to fit in at one time. There's Mary, the mother of John Mark, in whose house the church gathered to pray for the imprisoned Peter (Acts 12:12). There's also Priscilla and Aquila (1 Corinthians 16:19) and Apphia and Archippus (Philemon 1:2) who housed churches. This may have likely been true also of Chloe (1 Corinthians 1:11).

As with most families today, we can bet that the wives saw to the hospitality of their guests. Early Christians often met together for meals, and as we can see from 1 Corinthians 11:20, meals were sometimes a part of the worship gathering which was why Paul rebuked the Corinthians. Larry Hurtado, a scholar of Christian origins, wrote that when one considered the furniture in the average Roman home in antiquity, most Roman villas could have held no more than forty or fifty people if the atrium was used.[4] For these women to have held churches in their homes indicates that they had means. Moreover, they likely were wealthy enough to have servants who would have served and cleaned up afterward (cf. Acts 12:13). Imagine how you feel after hosting Thanksgiving or Christmas dinner. That's a lot of work! Yet, these women bore the responsibility of providing a place where the church could meet.

BEWARE

As with anything, there are certainly warnings for the church, or Christian, who would give and receive patronage. There is always a tendency when people give money to believe that they have a right to dictate the terms of how the funds should be stewarded. In fairness, if I gave a large sum of money, I'd certainly want to ensure that it was used appropriately. This is why due diligence should be performed prior to endowing another person or institution with any money. However, once I've given, I need to realize that I've given. If an individual or group chooses to use those funds in an unwise manner, I'm not obligated to give again.

A preacher friend of mine told me a horrific story. A rather wealthy family gave a large sum—six figures—to the church where he preached. I thank God for the elders' wisdom in this. They opened a special account just for this generous donation. They asked if there was any particular use the family would like to see those funds go towards. Later on, the elders of this congregation decided that they would install a screen for PowerPoint for the sermons and songs. This family accused the elders of misusing the funds and demanded the funds be returned. In the meantime, this family sowed discord within the church and actually caused a small split. The elders showed this family that they had put these particular funds in its own account and showed the checks that had been written from that account. The family, lacking good sense and any sort of Christian decency, persisted in accusing the elders of misusing the funds. The elders then wrote a check for the entire amount back to this family, and the family left while the church had paid money out of this account for good works.

In my opinion, I think that family just wanted to deduct a significant sum off their taxes. Otherwise, they could have written the checks on their own and supported good works. Yet, because churches are classified as a not-for-profit, people can deduct their donations on their tax returns and maybe even lower their own tax bracket and not have to pay as much in taxes to the government. Maybe I'm wrong, but I just can't see an actual Christian doing this. The love of money is surely the root of all evil.

So I issue this friendly warning to one who might be wealthy and chose to give their wealth for God's glory and the Gospel's use: examine your heart. If you're offering to bless, go ahead. However, if the one to whom you give misuses those funds, remember what Paul wrote about lawsuits among Christians, "Why not rather suffer wrong? Why not rather be defrauded?" (1 Corinthians 6:7). Money is that treasure that moths and rust will destroy and that thieves will break in and steal. Don't let your heart be in that treasure. To the recipient, I'd also say that you have the responsibility to present yourself as transparent as possible. If you receive funds, you have a responsibility to use them as they are intended. Otherwise, you are the unwise steward.

CONCLUSION

It may be tempting to think of the patroness as a widow, but that isn't always the case. A married woman can be a patroness too. However, if you've been graced with God's material blessings in this life, you have the opportunity to put it to good use. There may be a missionary who needs supporting. There may be a good work that needs funding. There very well may be an orphan that needs caring for. Even your own preacher may have a need that you might be able to fill.

One year around Christmas, one of the elders of the church where I attended called me aside into a private room. There I was in my early twenties with a wife and young daughter. The elder handed me an envelope, and in it was a check for several hundred dollars from the church. The elder told me that someone had done well that year in business and wanted to bless others. I wasn't starving and was making it just fine. But that money meant a lot to me. I never knew who gave it, because they wanted to remain anonymous. However, if they happen to read this, I've never forgotten your kindness. I'll forever be grateful.

Over the years, because of that gift, I have endeavored to do the same. I'm not rich, but I'm far from poor. I have been so glad to have anonymously given to others whom we knew were in need. We have also been glad that God has been extra generous to us so that we could enjoy the blessing of giving. It truly is more blessed to give than receive.

QUESTIONS

1. What are some pitfalls of being a patron of others? How can people who support good works balance good stewardship with not being controlling with their money?

2. Why don't more women open their homes today for hospitality?

3. How might women of today compare to women of antiquity and even their own grandmothers in how they cared for others when they could?

4. Are women today more selfish?

NOTES

1. *Interpretation of the Letter to the Romans.* Cf. Acts 18:18.

2. See Esther Yue L. NG, "Phoebe as Prostatis," *Trinity Journal* 25, no. 1 (Spring 2004): 3–13. A most helpful read to understand female patronage as a whole would be R. A. Kearsley, "Women in Public Life in the Roman East: Iunia

Theodora, Claudia Metrodora, and Phoebe, Benefactress of Paul," *Tyndale Bulletin* 50 (1999): 189–211.

3.   William Barclay, *The Gospel of Luke*, rev. ed. (Philadelphia: The Westminster Press, 1975), 97.

4.   Larry Hurtado, *At the Origins of Christian Worship: The Context and Character of Earliest Christian Devotion* (Grand Rapids: Wm. B. Eerdmans Publishing Company, 1999), 41.

8

DEACONESS

The order of the widows continued until the fourth century and began declining from that point on. The order that officially arose to replace them was that of the deaconess. This class is somewhat akin to their male counterpart, deacons. However, there were some differences. In the first century, the first episode of deacon ordination is believed to have been in Acts 6 when men were chosen to wait tables. After that, some of those men are evangelizing and baptizing among other works. Given that women could not have a public preaching or teaching role with males subordinated under them, their responsibilities would have differed from their male counterparts. They served, and they served well. In their time, deaconesses had a vital role in the life of the church.

DEACONESSES IN THE NEW TESTAMENT?

Two passages in the New Testament are usually argued to have been descriptive of the deaconess—Romans 16:1 and 1 Timothy 3:11. In the former, Phoebe is called a "servant" of the church.

The term translated "servant" in most English Bibles is *diákonon* in Greek. Now, if you remember your high school Spanish, you know that *señor* is how you address a man. *Señorita* is how you address a woman. That "a" at the end of the word indicates a female. In Greek, there were genders in words as well. *Diákonon* is feminine, so you could literally translate it as "deaconess." However, what's a matter of debate is whether the term was technical in the first century or general. Before you become worried, our English Bibles have not been mistranslated. The term is "servant." What trips us up is that few people know that deacons are servants. The terms "deacon," "servant," and "minister" are all synonymous. It's as scriptural to call a "deacon" a "servant," as it would be to call a "minister" a "deacon." Those words mean the same things. Our English Bibles translate the term "servant" because most scholars believe that the order of the deaconess was not organized until the third century. We'll talk about this more in a little bit, so hold on.

First Timothy 3:11 is translated as either "wives" or "women." You're probably wondering why those Greeks couldn't use appropriate words so that we could get what they meant. The term from which these words are translated is *gunaĩkas* or *gunē*. Our English word "gynecology" comes from this root. This term can be translated as either "wife" or "woman." The term is translated as "wife" when it's in direct relation to a man and usually connected by a possessive pronoun such as "your" or "their." Since no possessive pronoun appears, the New American Standard translators have accurately translated it as "women." However, the others translate it as "wives" because the verse is tucked within the description of the deacon. Paul began this description in 1 Timothy 3:8 and concluded in v. 13. Since v. 11 is tucked within the context of the deacon, the translators believe it to refer to the deacons' and overseers' wives. Now do you see how tough a job it is to translate?

Hopefully, you haven't fallen asleep during this Greek lesson. Let's get back on point. Both of these verses could be indicative of the office of the deaconess. I'll also go on and inform you that later commentators on the Bible in early Christianity debated whether these passages referred to deaconesses or not. On the passage about Phoebe, here is a sample of commentaries:

> This passage teaches that there were women ordained in the church's ministry by the apostle's authority.... Not only that—they ought to be ordained into the ministry, because they helped in many ways and by their good services deserved the praise even of the apostle. (Origen)

> Note how many ways Paul dignifies Phoebe. He mentions her before all the rest and even calls her his sister. It is no small thing to be called the sister of Paul! Moreover, he has mentioned her rank of deaconess as well. (John Chrysostom)

> In fact the church at Cenchreae was so large that it even had a woman deaconess, and one who was famous and well known to boot. (Theodoret of Cyr)[1]

On 1 Timothy 3, here's a sampling of commentaries:

> Some have thought that this is said of women generally, but it is not so, for why should he introduce anything about women to interfere with his subject? He is speaking of those who hold the rank of deaconesses. (John Chrysostom)

Paul does not refer here to women deacons, since these are not allowed in the church. It is heretics who have such persons. The reference here is to women in general. (Ambrosiaster)[2]

There was a general consensus on the passage about Phoebe that she was, in fact, a deaconess. From 1 Timothy, however, there was a little contention on that passage. Clement of Alexandria believed that Paul mentioned "women deacons" in his second letter to Timothy (*Strom.* 3.6.53), but he did not specify which passage he meant. Considering all of these facts, let's look to another source that isn't biblical.

Pliny the Younger was the governor of Pontus and Bithynia from AD 111–13. He exchanged letters with Emperor Trajan on a variety of issues, but one of his letters details when he met Christians for the first time.

Meanwhile, in the case of those who were denounced to me as Christians, I have observed the following procedure: I interrogated these as to whether they were Christians; those who confessed I interrogated a second and a third time, threatening them with punishment; those who persisted I ordered executed. For I had no doubt that, whatever the nature of their creed, stubbornness and inflexible obstinacy surely deserve to be punished.[...]Accordingly, I judged it all the more necessary to find out what the truth was by torturing two female slaves who were called deaconesses. (*Letters* 10.96)

There's much that could be said about Pliny's letters, but we'll stick to the point. When he wrote to the emperor, he noted that he had tortured two female slaves who were called "deaconesses." Again, we are not sure whether this was a technical term or a general term. Pliny's letter was translated from Latin, and the word used here is the one from which we get our word "minister"—*ministrae*. "Deaconess" is an appropriate translation, but so is "servant."

Here's what I believe—the office of "deaconess" isn't described until the third-century work *Didascalia*. Then, it was an office within Christianity. Before then, I believe the term was generally used and not as an official church office. Whether it was or wasn't has no bearing on what these Christian women did. What they did not do was teach and preach publicly even when the office was established, because that was—as Ambrosiaster noted above—heretical.

DEACONESS IN CHURCH HISTORY

In *Didascalia* 16, the primary duties of the deaconess were to minister to other women in several ways. There were some houses where the deacon could not go because it was a house of women. The point in sending a deaconess was so that the heathen would not be offended by this, or so that nothing untoward could be accused of having taken place. Another task of theirs was to assist in baptizing and teaching women after baptism. They also aided with Christian women who were recovering from illnesses.

> In the first place, when women go down into the water, those who go down into the water ought to be anointed by a deaconess with the oil of anointing; and where there is no woman at hand, and especially no deaconess, he who baptizes must of necessity anoint her who is being baptized. But where there is a woman, and especially a deaconess, it is not fitting that women should be seen by men?[...]And when she who is being baptized has come up from the water,

let the deaconess receive her, and teach and instruct her how the seal of baptism ought to be unbroken in purity and holiness. For this cause we say that the ministry of a woman deacon is especially needful and important. For our Lord and Saviour also was ministered unto by women ministers, Mary Magdalene, and Mary the daughter of James and mother of Jose, and the mother of the sons of Zebedee [Matt 27:56], with other women beside. And thou also hast need of the ministry of a deaconess for many things; for a deaconess is required to go into the houses of the heathen where there are believing women, and to visit those who are sick, and to minister to them in that of which they have need, and to bathe those who have begun to recover from sickness.[...]But let a woman rather be devoted to the ministry of women, and a male deacon to the ministry of men.

We might conclude that one reason for deaconesses was for the sake of propriety. As a male preacher, I have certain personal rules when interacting with the opposite sex. First of all, I have these rules because I made a promise to God and my wife, and I would never want to break my promise or be accused of impropriety. Secondly, I'd never want there to be any suspicion that I had broken my marital vows because I was ministering to a woman. I've heard of too many church leaders losing their influence because they acted irresponsibly towards the opposite sex. I'd say that it's been a blessing to have a supportive wife. It's even better to have supportive Christian sisters who could minister better in a setting that requires it so that nothing inappropriate could even be suspected.

Maybe one way you might serve the church is as one of these women who ministered to other women. I would be grateful to be able to turn to mature, spiritually-minded Christian sisters who could either be there while I had to counsel women. I'd be even more grateful to be able to give a name to one of these sisters who could go study the Bible with them and help teach them the will of God.

CONCLUSION

As church history progressed, adult baptism began to decline. The theology of the church believed in original sin and warranted that infants be baptized. Since the deaconess aided females in baptism—due to people in antiquity being baptized in the nude—their primary responsibility eroded and so did their order.

QUESTIONS

1. If you had to argue either way, how might you make a case that Phoebe either was or wasn't a deaconess in the sense of holding a church office?

2. Was there anything wrong with the office of deaconess that might contradict the Scriptures?

3. Would it be wrong to create an office today in the church for a certain purpose as long as it didn't go against God's commands?

4. How might women serve in the capacity as a deaconess without a title or office today?

NOTES

1. Bray, *Romans*, 369.

2. Gorday, *Colossians, 1–2 Thessalonians, 1–2 Timothy, Titus, Philemon*, 175–176.

9

WOMEN WHO PAID THE ULTIMATE PRICE

Today is a fitting day for me to write this chapter. It's Saturday, July 4th. When I reflect on America's history, you and I are both indebted to those who've given the ultimate sacrifice, by God's grace, to establish and preserve these United States of America. We Americans are certainly grateful to our soldiers and their families for the sacrifices they make. I'm grateful to know many good brethren who are or have served. Looking back, not only on our country's rich history but on Christianity's rich history, there have been men and women who've paid the ultimate price. They were convicted that to obey Christ is better. To say, "Lord Christ," rather than "Lord Caesar," was preferable. Because, as Paul wrote, our citizenship is in heaven (Philippians 3:20).

THE PLACE OF MARTYRDOM IN THE EARLY CHURCH

Beginning with Stephen in Acts, the persecution of Christians would not cease until Constantine became emperor. To die for a cause greater than one's self was the epitome of love (cf. John 15:13).

To make the ultimate sacrifice was to walk in love as Christ walked (Ephesians 5:2). Jesus left an example that many early Christians mirrored. They willingly gave their lives for the sake of the cross. Many Christians defected from the faith, but those who withstood the evil brought upon them would receive a heavenly reward that somehow became practical to celebrate on earth. The widespread martyrdom eventually led to identifying a particular class of Christians as "saints," because the early church believed that the holy dead participated in praying for the living.

Some believe that the veneration of martyrs did not originate with pagan sources and the hero cults, but with Jewish sources. In the *Hymns of Thanksgiving* contained in the Dead Sea Scrolls, one particular hymn reads in part, "Thou wilt raise up [the just man's] glory from among flesh."[1] Another source from the Intertestamental Period also seems to suggest that the faithful dead intercede in prayer on behalf of the living (2 Macc. 15:12).

The early church viewed the entire church, alive and dead, as one body. The first account of a celebration of a martyr in the early church was that of Polycarp, a student of the apostle John.[2] The early Christians cremated the body of Polycarp and saved his bones. The birthday, or day of martyrdom, was celebrated by a gathering that commemorated his sacrifice with those in mind that had already suffered a similar fate, as well as those who would do so in the future.

The commemoration of martyrs resulted in a cultic form of worship that was incorporated into Christian worship. The belief came to be that these martyrs were baptized by fire and blood, so they received an immediate entrance into heaven regardless of whether they had been previously baptized. Tertullian advocated that a martyr bypassed the intermediate state (Hades) and entered heaven immediately upon their sacrifice. Origen and Cyprian believed that the martyrs' prayers before the throne of God were most efficacious because of their martyrdom. As this practice became more readily accepted, the images of these martyrs were placed on curtains, stone, and various other materials so that one could venerate the picture. Prior to the advocacy of venerating the martyrs (or saints), several folks opposed to the practice. Canon 36 of the Council of Elvira (fourth-century) prohibited such recognition of visible emblems. Epiphanius of Salmis tore down a curtain within a Palestinian church that depicted the image of Christ or a martyr. He led a protest against the bishop at Jerusalem, but his war against the adoration never found solid ground.[3] By the fifth century, the practice was common to venerate the images of the saints.

EARLY FEMALE MARTYRS

Given the esteem of the martyrs at the beginning of Christianity, we now turn to highlight a few and their stories. These martyrdoms occurred during the reign of Marcus Aurelius in the second century (c. 161–80) except for Perpetua and Felicity whose sacrifices took place during the first years of the third century. Aurelius' persecution of Christians heightened during AD 166–68 when the empire was fighting the Parthian war and also receiving pressure from Germans. To top off Rome's troubles, an outbreak of plague arose as well around the same time. There might have been an edict that urged sacrifices to the gods, and this made Christians suspect due to their absence at the Roman altars. Aurelius did, however, praise the Christians in his only reference to them in his *Meditations*—"The resolute soul: Resolute in separation from the body. And then in dissolution or fragmentation—or continuity. But the resolution has to be one of its own decision, not just in response to outside forces [like the Christians]. It has to be considered serious, persuasive to other people. Without dramatics" (11.3). His reference to Christians shows just how resolute they were in the face of bodily harm—many of them women.

We'll begin with Felicitas of Rome, who was martyred in a circumstance that most women could not and would not tolerate. If you're a Christian mother, you don't want to miss this story! Felicitas was a widow and tiresome worker for the church and was the mother of seven sons. The pagan priests appealed to Marcus Aurelius because of her, so they rounded her and her seven children up. They questioned them and tried to get them all to deny their faith in Christ, but under the threat of torture and death, they would not deny the faith. Felicitas and her sons were sentenced to death, but Felicitas began praying that she would not be put to death before her sons. She was the last to be martyred, and during the time of her sons' torture and execution, she encouraged them to be faithful to God, knowing that they had a greater reward beyond the physical life. There are doubts about the entirety of this story of Felicitas, but there seems to be a consensus that she and her seven sons were martyred despite some details being questionable. This story reminds me of Hannah in 1 Samuel. She prayed to God for a son and then gave him to the temple service to be raised by Eli. I can't imagine watching my two children suffer, let alone seven if I had them. Perhaps this speaks to our perspective as parents. We all need the solidarity of heart even for our children's faith. Felicitas mothered her boys, literally, from the cradle to the grave.

Blandina at Lyons was a well-known female martyr in early Christianity. She was a slave whose master was also a Christian. Both were thrown into prison where they'd meet their martyrdom. Blandina was recorded to have had a frail body, but she was faithful under torture. Those appointed to her physical chastisement were so cruel and harsh that they became exhausted by torturing her. Blandina, however, was so faithful under chastisement that her torturers did not know what more they could do to her and actually were beaten by her solidarity. She is recorded to have replied to every question asked of her under torture, "I am a Christian, and we commit no wrongdoing."

She was eventually bound to a stake in the amphitheater and made to suffer more as wild beasts were loosened to devour her. Blandina is recorded to have prayed for the other Christians who were suffering torture. Eusebius quoted a source that said that those who saw her suffering and praying believed that they saw "in the person of their sister the One who was crucified for them" (*Eccl. Hist.* 5.1). Can you imagine a person's character so faithful to God that you feel as if you're looking at a modern saint? I remember one sister once remarking to me about the late Jim Bill McInteer, "This is like being with the apostle Paul." What a compliment! Some Christians are so godly that their lives are living examples to us as to how we should live as Christians.

Blandina's suffering was so great that even the heathens admitted to having never known of women who were able to suffer so much for such an extended period. Many of the others who were tortured with her had died before she did, so she had seen most of her brethren die for Christ. Yet, Eusebius leads us to believe that she prayed over them and cared for them more so than herself—as a loving mother. When most of them had passed, she finally died while rejoicing and exulting as if, Eusebius recorded, she was "invited to a wedding supper." It's certainly no doubt that her own strength, that of a woman, in such a horrific time encouraged those with her. The solidarity of her profession of faith was so unwavering that it gave courage to the others to remain untouched by their physical suffering.

Blandina is certainly a hero for us today. She was just an everyday slave-girl, but she died a monument of Christlikeness. We now turn to another Christian sister who gave her life for her faith, Perpetua. However, you can't talk about Perpetua without talking about Felicity, another slave-girl. You can read about their martyrdom in its entirety in the *Passion of Perpetua and Felicitas*.

Perpetua was a noblewoman whose father was pagan. Her dad

tried to encourage her to avoid Christianity. She had visions of her martyrdom in which it was said that she "became a man" in the arena—a reference to her strength. She was a young mother when she was martyred and had given her son to her pagan father to raise. As she and others entered the arena for their martyrdom, Perpetua is recorded to have begun singing psalms. She was stripped naked and led to the arena along with a slave-girl named Felicity, who was also a Christian. When their naked bodies were exposed to the crowd, the crowd saw that Perpetua was young (22 years old) by her nakedness. They also noticed that milk dripped from Felicity's breasts due to a recent childbirth. The onlookers demanded that they be clothed—perhaps to ease their consciences. When they were returned dressed, they were left in the arena with a wild heifer that mauled them. Their battered bodies were put on a platform where they were eventually executed.

CONCLUSION

May the day never come when we must face martyrdom. However, should it come, may we all be as resolute as these godly women were. When you read this chapter, how important is your faith to you? These stories really make me wonder if Christian women, or men for that matter, are as secure in their faith as they seem. This actually makes us prioritize what's crucial, and not what's just superficial.

QUESTIONS

1. Are we as Christians too attached to our families? If so, how might it be unhealthy when put in the view of our faiths?

2. Do we value the sacrifice of others in service to God as much as we should? Compare this to the value of sacrifice we have for those who are in the armed forces.

3. How important is it for women to have other women that they can admire or look up to as in the case of these mentioned here?

4. How prepared are we to sacrifice for Christ? Will we sacrifice our children's happiness, our family's vacations, etc.?

NOTES

1. Geza Vermes, trans., *The Complete Dead Sea Scrolls in English*, rev. ed. (London: Penguin Books, 2004), 256. See the argument made by Eric Werner in "Traces of Jewish Hagiolatry," in *Hebrew Union College Annual*, no. 51 (1980): 39-60.

2. *Martyrdom of Polycarp* 18.

3. See Philip Schaff *History of the Christian Church* 2.2.27; and Henry Chadwick, *The Early Church*, rev. ed. (London: Penguin Books, 1993), 281.

10

A DESPERATE HOUSEWIFE

Up until this point, we've focused on ways that women served in early Christianity. I've tried to highlight the good of these sisters and what they did in service to Christ and His bride—the church. I have wanted to keep this work positive and encouraging to you. However, I realize that sometimes the positive views of how women serve may lead some to believe that innovating and going a little farther is permissible when it might not be. Truthfully, in some things it is, but in others, it would be unwise. For this chapter and the next one, I want to highlight from church history some women who were considered to be apostate—that is, they were unfaithful heretics.

The woman that we'll discuss in this chapter wasn't necessarily a heretic herself, but her story was framed in such a way that she was unsound to many. Were you to read the account yourself, you'd likely fall in love with her, though. She was a woman who sacrificed a lot for her faith in God so that she could serve him. Who could hate that, right? Well, it's not that I want anyone to hate this woman that we'll study, Thecla. However, we must reign in our own desires and not let sensationalism or fancifulness take us captive so that we'd find pleasure in something that God might not. Before we can get to the heart of the matter, a little background work is necessary.

SPURIOUS WRITINGS

The New Testament was not the only group of books circulated in early Christianity. There were many works that were considered when the New Testament was formed, and some were almost included in the New Testament. However, when all things were considered, several key points went into deciding which works would be accepted and which would not be included in the New Testament canon. Three criteria were (1) apostolicity. Was the letter written by an apostle, or one closely associated with an apostle (e.g. Mark, Luke)? (2) Did the work follow the rule of faith? The rule of faith was the oral summary of doctrines born from Scripture. (3) Was the work universally accepted? That is, did the church in Jerusalem regard the same works as the churches in Rome and Alexandria? If a work conformed to the first two and enjoyed a universal appeal, it was believed to have been inspired by God.

One writing the early Christians enjoyed reading that wasn't canonized was *The Shepherd of Hermas*. There were many others. However, there were some writings that were not exactly kosher and that the early Christians believed were actually heretical—teaching false doctrine. Some of those writings believed to have taught false doctrine were mentioned by the church historian, Eusebius. "Among Spurious Books must be placed the 'Acts' of Paul" (*Eccl. Hist.* 3.25). In fairness, at the time Eusebius made his list he also included the book of Revelation. He added the caveat that some accepted Revelation as a "Recognized Book" while others did not. Revelation was eventually included, but not without a bit of a struggle. That's a discussion for another time.

Eusebius went on to write about the "Spurious Books":

> Again, nothing could be farther from apostolic us-
> age than the type of phraseology employed, while
> the ideas and the implications of their contents are
> so irreconcilable with true orthodoxy that they stand
> revealed as the forgeries of heretics. It follows that so
> far from being classed even among Spurious Books,
> they must be thrown out as impious and beyond the
> pale. (Ibid.)

To him and the church, some books were questionable, like
Revelation, while others were emphatically false. Those that were
categorically wrong stood against what Christianity stood for.

The books often rejected by the early church has of later decades
been included as a part of the entire narrative of Christianity. Liberal
scholars, some of whom are agnostic and even atheist, have dissected
these books to promote their own agenda while teaching that they
were a part of the Christian story. In fairness, they were a part of the
Christian story, but an unflattering part by those considered orthodox.

The *Acts of Paul* consisted of three principal parts: (1) *The Acts
of Paul and Thecla*, (2) Paul's correspondence with the Corinthian
church that eventually led to the writing of *3 Corinthians*, and (3) the
Martyrdom of Paul. These books were rejected because their content
was fanciful. In one of the writings, Paul actually baptized a lion, so
you can see why these works might be dismissed. Not only that, a
heretical group called the Manichees accepted them, which also led
to the church rejecting it. It's the *Acts of Paul and Thecla* that we'll
focus on in this chapter, because Thecla did some things contrary to
what the church taught. Her story actually spurred others to follow
her example down a path of apostasy.

THE ACTS OF PAUL AND THECLA

In this writing, the apostle Paul went to Iconium after he fled Antioch. The story may be an attempt to fill in a gap in history that occurred somewhere in Acts 14:1–21, because it also mentions Demas (cf. 2 Timothy 4:10) and Hermogenes (cf. 2 Timothy 1:15). These details, and the fact that the author mentions that these two characters were hypocrites, fits in with the biblical narrative given to us by some of Paul's legitimate writings. Nevertheless, the apostle Paul was at the house of Onesiphorus (cf. 2 Timothy 1:16; 4:19)—another historical character in Paul's legitimate writings. While preaching to the church that met in Onesiphorus' home, Paul begins preaching the Beatitudes from Jesus' Sermon on the Mount (*Acts of Paul and Thecla* 1.12–21).[1] In this writing, Paul added a beatitude for the virgins.

> Blessed are the bodies and souls of virgins; for they are acceptable to God, and shall not lose the reward of their virginity; for the word of their (heavenly) Father shall prove effectual to their salvation in the day of his Son, and they shall enjoy rest for evermore. (*Acts* 1.22)

This is the point in the narrative when Thecla is introduced. She was betrothed to a man, but was a virgin. Her betrothed, Thamyris, and her mother appear to her. She had sat outside at a window of Onesiphorus' house and had listened to Paul preach while she fasted. When Thamyris and Thecla's mother appear to her and greeted her, she ignored them and we're told that they felt that one lost his spouse while the other lost her daughter (cf. Luke 12:52–53; 14:26–27). Where the story contradicts Paul's teaching is that Demas and Hermogenes report that Paul "deprives young men of their (intended) wives, and virgins of their (intended) husbands, by teaching, There can be no future resurrection, unless ye continue in chastity, and do not defile your flesh" (*Acts* 2.16; cf. 4.2). This statement is wholly contradictory to Paul's teaching on marriage (1 Corinthians 7; 1 Timothy 4:1–3).

Subsequently, Paul was thrown in jail by Thamyris, who happened to be an influential person in Iconium. Thecla came to visit Paul in prison, and there the apostle taught her. Paul and Thecla were separated for a time—Thecla facing execution but being protected by God. They reunited and Thecla remained with Paul until she was taken by a man in a city who kissed her. She then rejected him, which landed her before the governor who threatened to throw her to the beasts. She averted this danger just as the previous attempt on her life. Through these narratives, she's shown to have been a pious virgin who had dedicated herself to God and rejected any thought of marriage.

She once again reunited with Paul, and after her "adventures," she made a couple of statements that would have been wholly rejected by the early church.

> I have been baptized, O Paul; for he who assists you in preaching has assisted me to baptize. (*Acts* 10.2)

> Then Thecla arose, and said to Paul, I am going to Iconium. Paul replied to her: Go, and teach the word of the Lord. (*Acts* 10.4)

These statements that a woman preach the Word and baptize were contrary to the church's customs. Thecla, after baptizing herself, cut her hair and dressed like a man before being commissioned by Paul. Of course, there was much that was contrary to New Testament teaching by this time, but these represent an entire departure from what Paul had taught in his other letters about women preaching

(1 Corinthians 14:33–35; 1 Timothy 2:11–14). Thecla is recorded to have gone along and taught (*Acts* 10.11) and worked many miracles (*Acts* 10.17).

Of course, it would be unjust to not mention the close of her story. In the last verses of this work, Thecla remained a virgin and devoted herself to the monastic life. She was eventually martyred. Her feast day is September 24th for those who observe the liturgical calendar. This work not only extolled her virtues as a person, but it also highlighted the order of the virgins which I mentioned earlier.

This account of Thecla was referred to in church history in an unflattering fashion. Tertullian, a second- and third-century African theologian, wrote the following:

> But if the writings which wrongly go under Paul's name, claim Thecla's example as a licence for women's teaching and baptizing, let them know that, in Asia, the presbyter who composed that writing, as if he were augmenting Paul's fame from his own store, after being convicted, and confessing that he had done it from love of Paul, was removed from his office. For how credible would it seem, that he who has not permitted a woman even to learn with over-boldness, should give a female the power of teaching and of baptizing! "Let them be silent," he says, "and at home consult their own husbands." (*On Baptism* 17)

If Thecla actually lived in the first century, her story had made its rounds from Asia down to Africa and was used to justify women's leadership roles in the church. These were the very roles that Tertullian identified and repudiated in his polemic. The *Acts of Paul and Thecla* has been debated as to whether the work should be read as a rejection of the restrictions on women or if it should have been read for entertainment. Whatever the answer, this work was shrouded in controversy.

CONCLUSION

Literature was an excellent way to spread the message. We have the Holy Bible in written form. However, some things can be written with such conviction that they lead others astray. I've highlighted how the *Acts of Paul and Thecla* seemed to have a historical setting by mentioning biblical names and places, let alone timelines. I give to you a piece of advice given to me by a good friend, and wonderful preacher. When reading any book or work that isn't the Bible, "Eat the fish, and throw away the bones." There is some good to this work, but a few points of the work led some astray. Whenever you read something that isn't the Bible, remember to exercise good discernment.

QUESTIONS

1. Considering how Christianity elevated women in Roman society, does their rejection of women preachers contradict that elevation or is there another way this could be explained?

2. What makes a book spurious as opposed to useful? Compare some of the works that were almost canonized vs. those that were deemed heretical.

3. What can be admired about Thecla?

4. How much weight should early church writers carry in our understanding of sound doctrine?

NOTES

1. From this point onward, I'll refer to the *Acts of Paul and Thecla* as *Acts*—not to be confused with the Acts in our New Testament which isn't italicized.

11

GIRLS GONE WILD!

You might recall my mentioning an African theologian, Tertullian, towards the end of the last chapter. Tertullian is often thought of as the father of Latin Christianity since a significant amount of his writings originally appears in this language. He's also regarded as the founder of Western theology. Yet, during his later years, he joined a group whose founder believed that he received the Holy Spirit and was given a new revelation. The name of this early Christian group that was thought of as heretical were "Montanists" based on their founder, Montanus. Two of the primary leaders of this movement were two women—Priscilla and Maximilla. These two women were instrumental in the spreading of Montanist teachings. However, the orthodox teachers noticed that their mode of operation was less than kosher. They were serving in roles for which God had not intended them. The church wasn't opposed to women prophets, but these two and their whole operation were anything but sound.

MONTANISM

Montanus was a pagan priest until he converted to Christianity in Phrygia. His group and their teachings were known to the church as the Phrygian heresy. Montanus claimed to have received the ecstatic prophesying ability from the Holy Spirit. A part of his claim was that his preaching and the work he did ushered in a new age. However, the ecstatic component of his work was one of the first things that raised red flags for the faithful.

In Eusebius' records, he cites a letter from a person named Apolinarius, who contended with the Montanists. In Apolinarius' letter, he stated that Montanus did prophesy, but not in a way that was aligned with the church's practice of prophesying. Some thought Montanus was possessed, so they rebuked him for behaving in an unseemly way. Others, however, were excited over this believing that the Holy Spirit was in fact operating through Montanus. Sound familiar? There are people today who claim to be "slain in the Spirit" and prophesy. Don't you see how history repeats itself? The letter went on to say that Montanus persuaded to his side those close to the actual faith, two of whom were women "whom he filled with the sham spirit, so that they chattered crazily, inopportunely, and wildly, like Montanus himself" (*Eccl. Hist.* 5.16).

Here's something worth noting: the church didn't disbelieve in prophecy. They believed that there was an appropriate way to prophesy, and the Montanists were not abiding by that custom. What made this false prophecy in the eyes of the church partly hinges on Paul's understanding of the Spirit: "And the spirits of the prophets are subject to the prophets" (1 Corinthians 14:32 NKJV). The Montanists believed in an ecstatic, out of control prophesying, while the church at the time, based on Paul's teaching, believed that a person controlled themselves if they were true prophets. Something the Montanists also did was to ecstatically prophesy as a method of interpreting the Scriptures to their own ends. This whole "I don't have control over myself" approach that we see today was exactly what these folks were doing centuries ago. It wasn't right then, and it's not right now.

It may have been fitting that this group arose where it did. In Asia Minor, the Gospel of John was highly treasured as church history tells us that he had resided in Ephesus. Moreover, the book of Revelation was based in Asia Minor. This was also where Philip and his daughters (who were prophetesses) lived. It's likely that this history and John's Gospel speaking of the Paraclete were conducive to this movement having some success in the region. It also goes to show that some didn't rightly divide the word of truth and discern between error and emotionalism—another problem in modern Christianity.

The reason that the church could not accept this new revelation was based on the fact that they would have had to view the Gospel accounts as merely a filler in history. Since the Montanists preached a new age of new revelation, that meant that the Gospel accounts were incorrect and really were a place setting until dessert could be served. Also, the Paraclete was the Holy Spirit, who had already been given on Pentecost. There was really no need for this new revelation. However, as with all groups who want to gain a following, what better way than to claim that they have divine knowledge limited only to a few select, anointed members? We see this in Mormonism as well as some other charismatic movements. Whenever the "prophet" of the movement dies, God miraculously appoints someone new to carry the sect into this new and troublesome time.

Hogwash, I say! I would agree with the ancient church. When you study carefully the New Testament and what the inspired writers had to say about the purpose of the miraculous gifts, including prophecy, you must conclude that it was to confirm the preached message (cf. John 5; Mark 16:20; Hebrews 2:4). Since the message has been long established, any new supposedly inspired person is simply heretical.

PRISCILLA & MAXIMILLA

Not a whole lot is known about these two women. Scholars have debated whether or not they were co-founders of Montanism. However, it's generally agreed that they provided a great deal of the prophetic content for the sect. Of course, to those who were orthodox in their views, these two women were perceived as agents of Satan. Eusebius said as much in his historical account of Christianity. Tertullian, however, tried to defend them by stating that they had both been confirmed, along with Montanus, as legitimate prophets by the bishop of Rome until another person came along and dissuaded that evaluation.[1]

Others in the orthodox community held contempt for these two women prophets. Hippolytus, a third-century bishop of Rome, had a bit to say about these two women.

> But there are others who themselves are even more heretical in nature (than the foregoing), and are Phrygians by birth. These have been rendered victims of error from being previously captivated by (two) wretched women, called a certain Priscilla and Maximilla, whom they supposed (to be) prophetesses. (*Refutation of All Heresies* 8.12)

> The Phrygians, however, derive the principles of their heresy from a certain Montanus, and Priscilla, and Maximilla, and regard these wretched women as prophetesses, and Montanus as a prophet. (Ibid. 10.21)

It's one thing not to like someone, but to use an unflattering adjective isn't the Christian way. The early Christians made no bones about being critical of heretics. Of course, given society's view of women at that time, it may have been a little harsher for Priscilla and Maximilla. Lactantius, a late third-to-early-fourth-century Christian, served as an advisor to Emperor Constantine. In his work, *Divine Institutes*, he warned against heresies noting that they were instigated by demons. Among those mentioned were the Phrygians or Montanists (4.30).

I wouldn't have you to believe that, just because Priscilla and Maximilla prophesied, that should be the first indication of heresy. Good, faithful women prophesied as we have discussed earlier, but there was a particular way that the gift of prophecy was exercised in the early church. We know from earlier on that in the divine worship, women were to remain silent. Therefore, there must have been an orderly way for those sisters genuinely gifted with prophecy to exercise their gift to God's glory and not their own. These women, caught up with Montanus, prophesied and went along with false doctrine more than anything. Moreover, their supposed gift of prophecy was icing on the cake. Any time you see women going along with sensationalism and not respecting God's Word, you're looking at a girl gone wild.

HOW SHALL WE DISCERN?

Had this heresy existed during the dispensation of the Old Testament, the penalty would have been death. "But the prophet who presumes to speak a word in My name, which I have not commanded him to speak, or who speaks in the name of other gods, that prophet shall die" (Deuteronomy 18:20). In Jeremiah's day, many false prophets spoke, and God was not pleased with any of them because they claimed to speak in His name, all the while leading His people astray (Jeremiah 14:14; 23:31; 27:15). What made the Montanist prophets so persuadable was that they spoke in Jesus' name. But they will be among those to whom the Lord says, "Depart from me" (Matthew 7:23).

Anytime people claim some new insight or new revelation, their behavior is more telling about the truth of their claim than anything. People doubted Jesus, but even He submitted to the righteous standard of obeying God's prophet, John the Baptist, by being immersed though He was without sin. Moreover, in John 5, Jesus followed the Jewish custom and law by having several witnesses attest to His person rather than just relying on His personal testimony. If Jesus was so concerned with following God's revealed will, any person who claims to be from God would behave as God has already commanded in His Word. That these women spoke ecstatically and took a position of leadership shows that they had no interest in submitting to God's will as it regarded their sex. Rather, they were concerned with personal vanity.

It's true that the Montanist group had strict regulations that appeared to align with Christian disciplines. For example, they prohibited people to remarry following divorce or the death of a spouse. The latter is something that we've already discussed as being permissible, though not remarrying was preferred. The Montanists bound where they shouldn't have bound. They were even a little too strict on some of their teachings as I see it. They emphasized fasting and often introduced new fasts. They also gave their teachers salaries, which the orthodox did not allow. However, the appearance of godliness in traditions and disciplines can certainly be overshadowed by the blatant rejection of elementary principles shown in the Scriptures. That they allowed female bishops and elders—this was the church hierarchy at the time—was certainly a tell-tale sign of their heresy as far as the orthodox saw it.

CONCLUSION

Throughout the most of this work, we've highlighted the positive ways that women served the church. Many were selfless, but in these last two chapters we've looked at some rather selfish ways that women sought their own glory. Because they abandoned the commandments of God, they are deemed as unworthy examples of what Christian women should do and how they ought to conduct themselves. Let us learn from the mistakes and examples of failures from those who've committed them so that we can be who God wants us to be.

QUESTIONS

1. What made these women heretical?

2. Can women be associated with a great work of God and yet not violate His teachings on their role?

3. How did these women depart from orthodox custom?

4. What advice might you give to younger women who want to preach?

NOTES

1. *Against Praxeas* 1.

12

HOW FAR DID CHRISTIANITY TAKE WOMEN?

The way Jesus treated women totally rebuffed the way they were regarded by not only the Jews, but also the Romans. Was Jesus the first feminist? I don't think so. The modern women's movement sometimes exalts the woman while doing to the man what they feel has been done to the woman for centuries. Jesus saw the value in each man and woman. Jesus' humanism, we must argue, was based on the fact that He, as the Creator, fashioned them after His image and likeness (cf. Colossians 1:15–17).

Each person has intrinsic worth, but because humans are prone to err, women were treated in a way that God didn't intend. Therefore, in Christ, we see a radical shift in how women were viewed socially and religiously. This chapter will highlight how antiquity regarded women with the hopes that the reader will see just how far Jesus took our opinions towards women.

WOMEN IN GRECO-ROMAN SOCIETY

Nearly all of what we know about women in antiquity is from male-written sources. There were women who were well educated and could read and write. However, the purpose of them having this depth of education was not so much to be as educated and engaged as their male counterparts were in literature and politics. Rather, their literacy was typically so that they could primarily serve as guardians of their households and the affairs about the home. For the Greco-Roman woman, they were certainly masters of the house. They ran the home, despite the males being the heads of the homes—

> The things that we use only for festivals or entertainments, or on rare occasions, we handed over to the housekeeper, and after showing her their places and counting and making a written list of all the items, we told her to give them out to the right servants, to remember what she gave to each of them, and when receiving them back to put everything in the place from which she took it. (Xen. *Oec.* 9.10)

Granted, some women were poets and philosophers, but very few of their writings exist. Yet, some are still extant and taught in universities and feminist studies.

In Greek society, women/wives were often kept more in the home than they were allowed to be in public. Their "place", if you will, was to be women and to be in the home as reflected in some writings (e.g. Soph. *Ant.* 578ff). A part of the reason for this was to protect the legitimacy of their offspring since many women married at young ages and were prime for scandal. I'm talking early to mid-teens when they would marry—"Why, what knowledge could she have had, Socrates, when I took her for my wife? She was not yet fifteen years old when she came to me, and up to that time she had lived in leading-strings, seeing, hearing and saying as little as possible" (Ibid. 7.5).

Even as wives, sadly, not all were as treasured as we tend to emphasize in Christian thinking today. Greek and Roman men were married to women who bore them legitimate children, but these men also might have mistresses or concubines. If the mood struck them, they would fornicate with their male and/or female slaves. In ancient Greek culture, there were primarily two classes of people—the penetrators and the penetrated. Forgive the explicit nature of this comment, but I want you to understand just how far Christianity upheld the dignity of the woman. The penetrators were the highest class while the penetrated—be they women or male recipients of intercourse—were a lesser quality. Therefore, the more senior class could act however they wanted without fear of anything the lower class could do or say.

> For this is what living with a woman as one's wife means—to have children by her and to introduce the sons to the members of the clan and of the deme, and to betroth the daughters to husbands as one's own. Mistresses we keep for the sake of pleasure, concubines for the daily care of our persons, but wives to bear us legitimate children and to be faithful guardians of our households. (*Demosthenes* 59.122; ca. 382–322 BC)

> Avoid impurity to the utmost of your power before marriage, and if you indulge your passion, let it be done lawfully. But do not be offensive or censorious to those who indulge it, and do not be always bringing up your own chastity. (*Epic. Ench.* 33.8; ca. AD 55–135)

These two quotes show that the wife was only for the legitimacy of children, and men were at liberty to do as they saw fit. Women today would divorce such men, but it was rather common for men to have extramarital affairs in antiquity.

Roman women enjoyed greater privileges and were more public than Greek women. They still could not enter into politics and many weren't taught to write, so there's scarce information about Roman women other than what we may ascertain from male-written sources. Depending on a Roman woman's wealth and social status, she could exert a significant amount of influence despite having little to no power at all.

WOMEN IN JEWISH SOCIETY

When thinking about Jewish women, we have to understand that they enjoyed a measure of worth comparable, maybe a little better, than the Greco-Roman woman. They were viewed differently in all matters of legal, religious, and social standings just like their Greco-Roman counterparts. Yet, Jewish women weren't as restricted in public appearances, but they did not have as much freedom as a Roman lady.

Intertestamental literature paints a portrait similar to what we might see in the New Testament. Women had certain duties and work that only they did (Tobit 2:11). They too were typically categorized along with those of a lower social standing such as younger men and children (Judith 6:16; 7:23). For a woman to have a measure of worth in rabbinic Judaism, she had to bear children. Of the seven classes excommunicated from Heaven, one was a Jewish man who had a wife who bore him no children (*Pes.* 113b). Some took the thought further and suggested that the Jewish male who had no child was actually dead himself. This man was an equivalent to a corpse (*Ned.*

64b). These thoughts were reflective upon a Jewish male finding a good wife even though the responsibility to procreate rested with the husband more so than the woman. Yet, this demonstrates a social shunning about men based on their wives.

WOMEN IN CHRISTIANITY

I have purposefully portrayed the worst of these societies' views of women to contrast just how fair Christianity was and should continue to be. Even when we evaluate how Greco-Roman and Jewish society viewed women, their lot was not altogether horrible. They had many privileges in those societies and were anything but miserable. Yet, the mistreatment of women, or viewing them as anything less than how Christ did, goes only to show just how flawed human nature is in our quest to bring order into chaos.

Paul has often been regarded as a misogynist when his teachings about female silence in the church and Eve being the cause of the Fall are compared with Jesus' treatment of women. However, it was Paul who, in Galatians 3:28, wrote, "There is neither Jew nor Greek, there is neither slave nor free man, there is neither male nor female; for you are all one in Christ Jesus" (NASB). What may escape many readers' notice is the fact that this passage is in direct contradiction to a Jewish prayer where the male thanked God that he wasn't made a woman, slave, or Gentile (*b. Ber.* 13b). Paul bucked against the tide of his own upbringing by noting how all were equal in God's eyes. Yet, this still doesn't settle with those who believe that women should be elders and preachers. Paul's view here was theoretically based on the equality of believers, while his admonitions on silence and the Fall were to justify a function. He fully believed that women were equal, but that they were restricted from certain tasks that were reserved for men.

Paul even went so far with his views on women, as guided by

the Spirit, to state that the believing wife sanctified her unbelieving husband. If Paul were really the misogynist that he's painted to have been, then there would be no way that the woman could have ever done what he claims she could do in 1 Corinthians 7:14. As it was, she had the ability not only to sanctify her unbelieving husband, but also, he later wrote, she might be able to save him.

Christianity believed in women. When Jesus saw the woman in adultery, He knew the purpose of her being brought forth and that there was no man present. Honestly, she couldn't have committed adultery with herself! He didn't condemn her when the crowd wanted to. Christ told her to go and sin no more. Women even touched him—such as the woman with the alabaster flask—which was taboo. The Pharisee believed that Jesus wouldn't have let her touch Him if He really knew what kind of woman she was, a sinner. It was a Samaritan woman with whom Jesus spoke at the well. Women learned from Him and supported Him financially. Two women were the first to discover the empty tomb when a woman's testimony wasn't even permitted in a Jewish court of law. It was to these women that Jesus revealed Himself as risen Lord. Not men.

CONCLUSION

The value of women, as with any person, stems from the belief that humanity is made in the image of God (Genesis 1:26–27). As image-bearers of our Creator, we have been given worth that surpasses what anyone else could assign to us. Christ viewed people this way too (cf. Matthew 19:4; Mark 10:6). Because God has invested us with worth, we ought to treat everyone of any sex, race, social status, educational background, and any other demographic imaginable with the love of Christ Jesus.

So how far did Christianity take women? The portrait painted in antiquity isn't a full treatment on the subject, but Jesus once asked His disciples, "What more are you doing than others" (Matthew 5:47). That principle should be a guiding principle in the life of the Christian. It should inform how we regard others. Christianity took women out of the second class and gave them first class seats.

QUESTIONS

1. How far should progress go for women?

2. Has the modern church been responsible for valuing women, or have we gone in the opposite direction?

3. Has preaching on women's roles been reactionary to those who teach differently from us? If so, could we be guilty also of cherry-picking Scriptures?

4. Are modern feminists correct in asserting that Paul was a misogynist?

13

WHERE DO WE GO FROM HERE?

The case could easily be made that the cause of feminism is the cause of Christianity. How we might understand this thought might differ from others. Nevertheless, Jesus indeed acted contrary to the convention of His own time when He elevated women to the status of the disciple. Yet, we find that when He selected His apostles, they were all men.

Should we continue to advance the cause of women just like Jesus did? Was Paul's restrictions upon women a turn in the tide of rabbinical conservatism towards women? Where do we go from here?

PREACH A WELL-BALANCED DIET OF THE WORD

To my fellow ministers and proclaimers of God's Word, let us never neglect to teach the whole counsel of God. I have been guilty, as have some of you, of presenting the New Testament information about women from the negative view of what they cannot and should never do. The reason for this, I hope, is understandable. We're always contending against false teachers. Moreover, if we're about our Father's business as the young Christ was, we should be studying with the lost and leading them to Christ. Sometimes we have to do a whole lot of deconstructing of what people have learned or seen in denominations. But let's not forget that there's another side of the story.

We may well be guilty of having repressed our Christian sisters by our preaching. We can't unscramble the egg, but we can certainly do better the next time we cook. Some of the ways we can improve this is to be sure to always preach the opposite side of the story and not make it so one-sided, such as what women can't do as Christians. Expository preaching is perhaps a great aid to these ends. By going through books of the Bible, rather than picking passages disconnected from a book's context, we can highlight the good, bad, and ugly. I recently taught through Paul's letters to the Thessalonians. When I came to 1 Thessalonians 4:1–8, I must admit I was a bit embarrassed. The whole passage was about sexual purity. I would have never chosen that text to preach on, especially to an adult audience. However, I taught through it and was told by many older Christians that they know older preachers who would have avoided that passage and topic like the plague.

I truly hope that I've been fair to God's Word in this work. You may find sections here or there that you disagree with, so I only ask that you please keep in mind my own human frailty and the need I have for God's grace and wisdom. However, I wanted to present the positive side of a Christian woman's service. In my conversations with many Christian women, I've been met with looks of defeat. Our sisters are precious, and we need to remind them of that. Let's preach a well-balanced diet of the Word.

SEEK THE ANCIENT PATHS

Instead of society leading us, let's explore the ancient paths of God's ways. I still believe that the Restoration Plea is a valid plea today. Let's do what they did, and get what they got in the New Testament. Those ancient paths not only consisted of the women who were heroes of faith, but those old ways also consisted of men preaching and praying in every place. Women were simply not allowed to preach and teach in the church to the subordination of men.

Of lately, many churches have started down a path that concerns me. You may think it no problem that women serve on the Lord's Table, but the move opens the door for more that could lead to full-blown apostasy. I don't have all the answers, and I know the Bible doesn't address this particular move that many have made in the Lord's body. However, I'd like to know the motive for having women serving on the Lord's Table. From what I deduce, it seems to be a change where people are declaring we've had it so wrong for so long, and that they now want to show that it's right or okay. Sometimes it comes as a surprise to the congregation, and sometimes the leadership of a church announces that they're going to do it. Why? Do they announce it because God has commanded it, or because they want to flaunt their Christian liberty to do so? If it's for liberty's sake, please consider—

> Therefore let us pursue the things which make for peace and the things by which one may edify another. Do not destroy the work of God for the sake of food [or women waiting tables]. All things indeed are pure, but it is evil for the man who eats with offense. It is good neither to eat meat nor drink wine nor do anything by which your brother stumbles or is offended or is made weak. (Romans 14:19–21)

But beware lest somehow this liberty of yours become a stumbling block to those who are weak. (1 Corinthians 8:9)

It's clear that God hasn't commanded who shall wait at the Lord's Table. A part of the problem stems from the fact that early churches met in homes and the whole of the congregation wasn't pointed toward a pulpit.

From a pragmatic perspective, those who serve the supper usually preside or pray over it by giving thanks before we all partake. Is this something that God would allow a woman to do? I think not, for then the passage that says that the men should pray in every place would be transgressed (1 Timothy 2:8). Moreover, from a church history perspective, Justin Martyr wrote about the Lord's Supper that the President offered prayers and thanksgivings and the he made the distribution to the church. If any were absent due to illness, the deacons took them the supper so that they could partake as well (*First Apology* 67). The first deacons selected in Acts 6 though they're not named as deacons, waited ("deaconed") tables. In church history, serving on the Lord's Table may have been a primary function of the deacons as well as serving the tables of the widows.

I know that those brethren who make this move have the purest intentions. I've spoken with many of them, and they're fine people. However, I fundamentally disagree with them on this move. Not only do the Scriptures make women serving the Lord's Table problematic due to presiding over it, but church history seems to serve as a commentary to the New Testament by suggesting that it was in fact men who served the Lord's Table.

I'm wholeheartedly interested in preserving the ancient paths. Yet, I know there are some things that the Bible doesn't explicitly instruct us on. However, there are abiding principles from the Scriptures, and church history, that can aid our interpretation. The ancient paths are still worth pursuing. We need to follow the Bible before any and every other source.

PERSONAL REFLECTIONS

Those from the gender justice movement may have impressions of us just as we do with them. Both our and their impressions of one another may be based in fact or in myth. I sat in a group of scholars a few years ago and this topic of women in the church was raised, and I gave some input, only to be later passive-aggressively dismissed. I wasn't among those of my thinking, but those of the other persuasion. I even asked to be corrected or shown the right way if I erred. No one spoke up at that point, but the passive-aggressive dismissal came later.

I'm certainly interested in talking with our brethren who I feel have erred on this. But my discussion in no way implies that I will go along with the installment of women preachers or elders. I'm no enemy to women, I promise. I have a wife and daughter who could attest to this. I want for them to reach their utmost potential to God's glory. They both are convinced as I am of the overall principles described in this book. We understand those Bible passages the same way.

I guess what I'd like for anyone who differs from some of us to know is that we value women. We may have poorly communicated this, but we do. We want them to excel and be all that they could be. I admit that some would be content for all women to be barefoot and pregnant and in the home—but not all of us. Many of our wives have chosen to abandon salaries and prestige in the workplace so that they could devote themselves to their homes. My wife is such a woman. She had worked for a well-respected doctor at the top of his field in Nashville before we decided for her to come home to be a full-time mom and wife. Where might she after these nine years had she remained in that job? We'll never know, but we made the decision for her to stay home.

When she decided to go back to school to finish her degree, I was on board. I've been her greatest cheerleader, and I'm so proud of her for wanting to reenter the workplace since our children are both in school. Whatever she decided, I've supported. Whichever way she's wanted to go, I've been on board. We both want to honor God and bring up godly children. We both understand the Scriptures to communicate that she should never preach or teach publicly.

CONCLUSION

I exhort all of my sisters in love to go and be your own Phoebe. Serve Christ in any way you can and in any way that pleases Him. I cannot tell you how touched I've been by many great Christian women. I also can't tell you just how I've been formed as a Christian, husband, father, and man by so many women whom God has seen fit to put into my life. Where would the world be without Phoebe's? I shudder to think.

QUESTIONS

1. What are the advantages of certain styles of preaching vs. others?

2. How might early church's meeting in houses have eliminated some of the issues we face, such as women waiting on the table?

3. Should we avoid a practice if we know it may lead to other practices that eventually birth a departure from fidelity to God's will?

4. How can we better communicate to women their value in the church?

PERSONAL NOTES

PERSONAL NOTES

PERSONAL NOTES

PERSONAL NOTES

PERSONAL NOTES

PERSONAL NOTES

PERSONAL NOTES

PERSONAL NOTES

PERSONAL NOTES

PERSONAL NOTES

PERSONAL NOTES

PERSONAL NOTES

PERSONAL NOTES

Made in the USA
Charleston, SC
11 January 2017